EVERYMAN

AND OTHER PLAYS

By ANONYMOUS

Everyman and Other Plays
By Anonymous

Print ISBN 13: 978-1-4209-6077-8
eBook ISBN 13: 978-1-4209-5978-9

Cover Image: a detail of "Medieval mystery play", by Kenneth John Petts (1907-92) / Private Collection / © Look and Learn / Bridgeman Images.

Please visit *www.digireads.com*

CONTENTS

Introduction

By craftsmen and mean men, these pageants are played,
And to commons and countrymen accustomably before:
If better men and finer heads now come, what can be said?

The pageants of the old English town-guilds, and the other
mysteries and interludes that follow, have still an uncommon reality
about them if we take them in the spirit in which they were originally
acted. Their office as the begetters of the greater literary drama to
come, and their value as early records, have, since Sharp wrote his
Dissertation on the Coventry Mysteries in 1816, been fully illustrated.
But they have hardly yet reached the outside reader who looks for life
and not for literary origins and relations in what he reads. This is a pity,
for these old plays hide under their archaic dress the human interest that
all dramatic art, no matter how crude, can claim when it is touched with
our real emotions and sensations. They are not only a primitive
religious drama, born of the church and its feasts; they are the genuine
expression of the town life of the English people when it was still lived
with some exuberance of spirits and communal pleasure. As we read
them, indeed, though it be in cold blood, we are carried out of our
book, and set in the street or market-square by the side of the
"commons and countrymen," as in the day when Whitsuntide, or
Corpus Christi, brought round the annual pageantry to Chester,
Coventry, York, and other towns.

Of the plays that follow, six come from the old town pageants,
reflecting in their variety the range of subject and the contemporary
effect of the cycles from which they are taken. They are all typical, and
show us how the scenes and characters of the east were mingled with
the real life of the English craftsmen and townsfolk who acted them,
and for whose pleasure they were written. Yet they give us only a small
notion of the whole interest and extent of these plays. We gain an idea
of their popularity both from the number of them given in one town and
the number of places at which regular cycles, or single pageants, were
represented from year to year. The York plays alone that remain are
forty-eight in all; the Chester, twenty-four or five; the Wakefield,
thirty-two or three. Even these do not represent anything like the full
list. Mr. E. K. Chambers, in an appendix to his Mediæval Stage, gives a
list of eighty-nine different episodes treated in one set or another of the
English and Cornish cycles. Then as to the gazette of the many
scattered places where they had a traditional hold: Beverley had a cycle
of thirty-six; Newcastle-on-Tyne and Norwich, each one of twelve;
while the village and parochial plays were almost numberless. In Essex
alone the list includes twenty-one towns and villages, though it is fair

to add that this was a specially enterprising shire. At Lydd and New Romney, companies of players from fourteen neighbouring towns and villages can be traced in the local records that stretch from a year or so before, to eight years after, the fifteenth century.

Mrs. J. R. Green, in her history of Town Life in that century, shows us how the townspeople mixed their workday and holiday pursuits, their serious duties with an apparent "incessant round of gaieties." Hardly a town but had its own particular play, acted in the town hall or the parish churchyard, "the mayor and his brethren sitting in state." In 1411 there was a great play, From the Beginning of the World, played in London at the Skinner's Well. It lasted seven days continually, and there were the most part of the lords and gentles of England. No copy of this play exists, but of its character we have a pretty sensible idea from various other plays of the Creation handed down from the north-country cycles. In the best of them the predestined Adam is created after a fashion both to suggest his treatment by Giotto in the medallion at Florence, and his lineaments as an English mediæval prototype:—

> "But now this man that I have made,
> With the ghost of life, I make him glad,
> Rise up, Adam, rise up rade,[1]
> A man full of soul and life!"

But to surprise the English mediæval smith or carpenter, cobbler or bowyer, when he turns playgoer at Whitsuntide, assisting at a play which expressed himself as well as its scriptural folk, we must go on to later episodes. The Deluge in the Chester pageant, that opens the present volume, has among its many Noah's Ark sensations, some of them difficult enough to mimic on the pageant-wagon, a typical recall of the shipwright and ark-builder. God says to Noah:—

> A ship soon thou shalt make thee of trees, dry and light.
> > Little chambers therein thou make,
> > And binding pitch also thou take,
> > Within and out, thou ne slake
> > To anoint it thro' all thy might.

In the York Noah's Ark pageant, which seems to be the parent-play in England of all its kind, we have this craftsman's episode much enlarged. "Make it of boards," God says, "and wands between!"

---

[1] rade, quickly.

> Thus thriftily and not over thin,
> Look that thy seams be subtly seen
> And nailéd well, that they not twin:
> Thus I devised it should have been;
> Therefore do forth, and leave thy din

Then, after further instructions, Noah begins to work before the spectators, first rough-hewing a plank, then trying it with a line, and joining it with a gynn or gin. He says:—

> More subtilely can no man sew;[2]
> It shall be clinched each ilk and deal,
> With nails that are both noble and new,
> Thus shall I fix it to the keel:
> Take here a rivet, and there a screw,
> With there bow,[3] there now, work I well,
> This work, I warrant both good and true.

To complete the pedigree of this scene we must turn to the old poem, the "Cursor Mundi," which, written in the fourteenth century, the time when the northern miracle-plays were taking decisive shape, appears to have served their writers as a stock-book. The following passage is own brother to that in the York miracle-play:—

> A ship must thou needs dight,
> Myself shall be the master-wright.
> I shall thee tell how broad and long,
> Of what measure and how strong.
> When the timber is fastened well,
> Wind the sides ever each and deal.
> Bind it first with balk and band,
> And wind it then too with good wand.
> With pitch, look, it be not thin!
> Plaster it well without and in!

The likeness we see is startling: so near to the other indeed as to suggest almost a common authorship.

As for the pastoral plays in the same towns, we find the shepherds and countrymen were just as well furnished with rough cuts from the life. The most real and frankly illustrative, and by no means the least idyllic of them is perhaps the Chester play of the three shepherds. It

---

[2] sew, i.e. stitch on the planks together.
[3] "Bow"—the arched frame on which the ship is built.

was not played by countrymen but by townsmen, like the other plays in the town cycles, being in this case the "Paynters and Glasiors" play. The first shepherd who opens it talks of the "bower" or cote he would build, his "sheep to shield," his "seemly wethers to save:"—

> From comely Conway unto Clyde
> Under tildes[4] them to hide
> A better shepherd on no side
> No earthly man may have
> For with walking weary I have methought
> Beside thee such my sheep I sought
> My long-tail'd tups are in my thought
> Them to save and heal

In the Death of Abel, another Chester play, Cain comes in with a plough, and says:—

> A tiller I am, and so will I be,
> As my daddy hath taught it me
> I will fulfil his lore

In the subsequent incident of the corn that Cain is to offer for his sacrifice, we hear the plain echo of the English farmer's voice in the corn-market mixing with the scriptural verse: "This standing corn that was eaten by beasts," will do:

> God, thou gettest no better of me,
> Be thou never so grim

So throughout the plays the folk-life of their day, their customs and customary speech, are for ever emerging from the biblical scene.

In trying to realise how the miracle-plays were mounted and acted, we shall find the best witness at Chester. This was a rather late one. Archdeacon Rogers, who saw them in 1594, when they had been going on for something like three centuries in all. From his account (in the Harleian Miscellany) it appears the Chester plays were given on Whit-Monday, Tuesday, and Wednesday.

"The manner of these plays were, every company had his pageant or part, a high scaffold with two rooms, a higher and a lower, upon four wheels. In the lower they apparelled themselves, and in the higher room they played, being all open on the top, that all beholders might hear and see them." They were played, he goes on to say, in every street:

"They began first at the abbey gates, and when the first pageant

---

[4] tents

was played, it was wheeled to the high cross before the mayor, and so to every street. So every street had a pageant playing before it at one time, till all the pageants for the day appointed were played. When one pageant was near ended, word was brought from street to street, that so they might come in place thereof, exceeding orderly, and all the streets have their pageants before them, all at one time playing together, to see which plays was great resort and also scaffolds and stages made in the streets in those places where they determined to play their pageants."

The same writer explains elsewhere that these plays were divided into twenty-four pageants, according to the number of the city companies, and that each company brought out its own pageant.

At York, whose plays Miss L. Toulmin Smith edited in 1887, we can turn to Davies's two books[5] and the local records, to complete the Chester description. Those who travel to York by rail to-day, and there dismount, as most of us have often done, to walk through the city to the cathedral, will be interested to find that the railway station now stands where once was Pageant Green. Near it was formerly another kind of station, where stood the houses hired to keep the pageants stored and put away from one year's show to another. The word "pageant," (pagina, or plank), we ought to recall, was used for the stage, or wheeled car of two stories, before it was used for the show set forth upon it. Davies helps us, as we perambulate York to-day, to mark where the old pageants were performed in 1399, at twelve stations, which were fixed and stated beforehand. The first station was at the gates of the Priory of the Holy Trinity in Mickle Gate, and the pageants were moved on them in turn to places at Skelder Gate end, North Street, Conyng Strete, Stane Gate and the gates of the Minster, so to the end of Girdler Gate; while the last of all was "upon the pavement." But the stations were subject to change, and there was much competition among wealthy householders (one of whom may have been the Robert Harpham mentioned in a 1417 list) to have the pageant played before their windows. The highest bidder gained the coveted right.

Before the actual day came, a town-crier was sent round the city to proclaim the "banes" or banns.[6] Arms were forbidden: "We command that no man go armed in this city with swords ne with carlill-axes, in disturbance of the king's peace and the play, or hindering of the procession of Corpus Christi, and that they leave their harness in their inns, saving knights and squires of worship that ought to have swords borne after them!" The plays began betimes. We read that at York the players were to be ready "at the mid-hour betwixt the IVth and Vth of the clock in the morning." Finally, for the players themselves, care was

---

[5] Extracts from the Municipal Records of York, 1843, and Walks through the City of York.

[6] See Appendix C. for the "Chester Banns."

taken to secure good ones for the several parts. Sometimes a player doubled or trebled the characters in a particular play.

All through the XIVth and XVth centuries miracle-plays went on being performed regularly, or irregularly, in most of the English towns and larger villages. One of the smaller cycles was that of Newcastle-upon-Tyne, played at Corpus Christi, from 1426 onwards. The Three Kings of Cologne is mentioned in 1536, which the goldsmiths, plumbers, glaziers, and others were to play. Here the pageants were not movable ones, but were given at fixed points. No doubt some of the spots associated with the Whitsuntide "shuggy-shows" (as I remember them in my time) were originally show-grounds of the town pageants too. Only one play of the Newcastle series has survived, and that fitly enough, having regard to the Tyneside shipbuilding, is a shipwrights' play. Unluckily it has been so modernised that not a vestige of the local colour or Tyneside dialect remains.

We come now to the date and origin of these town pageants. Of the three chief cycles earliest mention is to be found at Chester, and it carries us doubtfully back to 1268. Sir John Arnway was mayor in that year, according to one account: but the name recurs pretty positively in 1327-8, and about that time Randall Higgenet, a monk of Chester Abbey, wrote the plays. But in the text handed down they are of a much later style of diction, and no doubt later in date than the Towneley or York series.

About the real origin of these plays there can be no question. They began in the churches as liturgy plays, which were given at the Christmas, Easter, and other festivals, illustrating in chief the birth, life, death and passion of Christ. We owe to Professor Skeat the recovery of some fragments of liturgical plays in Latin, which have been reprinted by Professor Manly, in his Specimens of the Pre-Shaksperean Drama. The earliest example there is may be dated as early as 967, an important landmark for us, as it is often assumed that we have no dramatic record of any kind in these islands earlier than the Norman Conquest. Another generation or two of research, such as the pioneer work of Dr. Furnivall and the Early English Text Society has made possible, and we shall distinguish clearly the two lines of growth, French and Norman, English and Saxon, by which the town-pageants and folk-plays of the fourteenth and fifteenth centuries came to a head. Then the grafting of the English pastoral on the church-play, after it had been carried out into the open town or market-place, may become clear. Then, too, one will know how charged with potential dramatic life was the mind of him who wrote that interlude in four lines of the "Three Queens and the Three Dead Men," which contains in it the essence of a thousand moralities.

1st Queen. I am afeard.
2nd Queen. Lo, what I see?
3rd Queen. Me thinketh it be devils three!
1st Dead Body. I was well fair
2nd Dead Body. Such shall thou be.
3rd Dead Body. For Godes love, be-ware by me!

These breathe, not a Norman, but an Anglo-Saxon fantasy, and they speak for themselves. But many tell-tale documents exist to mark the concurrent Norman and English development that went on in the English mediæval literature, and was seen and felt in the church and guild plays, just as it went on in the towns themselves. It finds at last its typical expression in an interlude like the Coventry Nativity-play, reprinted in this volume. Long before the miracle-play was written in the form it finally took, and about the time when William of Rouen, after much trouble with his son Robert culminating at the battle of Gerberoi, was about to return to England, the new opening in the church in this country became one to tempt poor foreign students of some parts and some ambition. Among these was a graduate of the University of Paris, one Geoffrey, known to us now as Geoffrey of St. Albans. He had been offered the post of master of the abbey school at that place, but when he arrived after some delay—due perhaps to his going to see a mystery play at Paris—he found the post filled up. He then made his way to Dunstable, and while there proved his spirit by getting up a miracle-play of "Sancta Katarina." He borrowed copes from St. Albans in which to dress the actors; unluckily a fire took place, and the costumes were burnt. Thereupon he seems to have rendered himself up as it were in pious pledge for their loss, for he became a monk. In 1119 he was elected abbot, and if we give him about twenty-one years in which to rise to that dignity, we can date the St. Katharine play at 1098 or 9. This passage in a life of that time is a clue to the further history of the religious play in England. Geoffrey's attempt to present one at Dunstable, no doubt a reproduction of one he had seen in France, is an instance of the naturalisation process that slowly went on.

The distinct break in the history of the miracle-play that made it from a church into a town pageant occurred about the close of the thirteenth century. From a performance within the church building it went on then into the church-yard, or the adjoining close or street, and so into the town at large. The clerics still kept a hand in its purveyance; but the rise of the town guilds gave it a new character, a new relation to the current life, and a larger equipment. The friendly rivalry between the guilds, and the craftsmen's pride in not being outdone by other crafts, helped to stimulate the town play, till at length the elaborate cycle was formed that began with sunrise on a June morning, and lasted until the torch-bearers were called out at dusk to stand at the foot of the pageant. ꜱ ᴛᴏᴘ

ꜱ ᴛᴀʀ ᴛ   The earliest miracle-plays that we can trace in the town cycles date back to the early years of Edward III. The last to be performed in London, according to Prynne, was Christ's Passion, which was given in James I.'s reign. It was produced "at Ely House, Holborn, when Gundomar lay there on Good Friday at night, at which there were thousands present." This was a late survivor, however, called to life by a last flicker of court sunshine on the occasion of the state visit of a Spanish ambassador. Here is an extreme range of over three centuries; and the old religious drama was still being performed in a more and more uncertain and intermittent fashion all through the dramatic reign of Shakspeare.

The ten plays that follow in this volume represent in brief the late remnant of this early drama, rescued at the point where it was ending its primitive growth, soon to give way to plays written with a consciously artistic sense of the stage. They are headed by the great and simple tragic masterpiece, in which they say their last word: the morality of Everyman, the noblest interlude of death the religious imagination of the middle ages has given to the stage. The two following Old Testament plays, The Deluge and the Sacrifice of Isaac, are the third and fourth pageants in the Chester series; played respectively by the Water-Leaders and Drawers of the river Dee, and by the Barbers and Wax-Chandlers. The next is from Coventry, a Nativity play, played by the Shearmen and Tailors. From the Wakefield series, preserved in the Towneley collection, we have three plays, the famous second shepherds' play, with the Crucifixion and the Harrowing of Hell, or extraction of souls from Hell (Extractio Animarum ab Inferno). Two Cornish mysteries of the Resurrection are included: The Three Maries at the Tomb, and Mary Magdalen bringing the News to the Apostles. Then follows Bishop Bale's oracular play of God's Promises, which is in effect a series of seven interludes strung on one thread, united by one leading idea, and one protagonist, the Pater Cœlestis.

In these religious and moral interludes, the dramatic colouring, however crude, is real and sincere. The humours of a broad folk-comedy break through the scriptural web continually in the guild plays like those in which Noah the shipbuilder, or the proverbial three shepherds, appear in the pageant. Noah's unwilling wife in the Chester Deluge, and Mak's canny wife in the Wakefield shepherd's play, where the sheep-stealing scenes reveal a born Yorkshire humorist, offer a pair of gossips not easy to match for rude comedy. Mak's wife, like the shepherd's in the same pastoral, utters proverbs with every other breath: "A woman's avyse helpys at the last!" "So long goys the pott to the water, at last comys it home broken!"

> Now in hot, now in cold,
> Full woeful is the household,
> That wants a woman!

And her play upon the old north-country asseveration, "I'll eat my bairn,"—

> If ever I you beguiled,
> That I eat this child
> That lies in this cradle,

(the child being the stolen sheep), must have caused towns-folk and country-folk outrageous laughter. Mak's wife is indeed memorable in her way as the Wife of Bath, Dame Quickly, or Mrs. Gamp.

There is nothing so boldly drawn in the Coventry Nativity. But there you have a startlingly realistic treatment joined to an emotional lyricism of the simplest charm:

> Neither in halls, nor yet in bowers,
> Born would he not be
> Neither in castles, nor yet in towers
> That seemly were to see.

and—

> As I outrode this enderes night
> Of three jolly shepherds, I saw a sight;
> And all about their fold a star shone bright,
> They sang "Terli, terlow!"
> So merrily the shepherds their pipes can blow.

In this Coventry play we have nearly all the ingredients—foreign, liturgical, or homely English—of the composite miracle play brought together. It bears traces of many hands; and betrays in the dialogue of the formal characters the rubricated lines of the church play on which it was based. The chief characters live, move and act their recognised parts with the certainty of the folk in a nursery tale. Herod out-Herods himself with a Blunderbore extravagance:—

> I am the cause of this great light and thunder;
> It is through my fury that they such noise do make.
> My fearful countenance, the clouds so doth incumber
> That oftentimes for dread thereof, the very earth doth quake.

"Fee, fi, fo, fum!" might be the refrain of this giant's litany. The other types are as plainly stamped. The shepherd's are from the life, and contrast well with the stilted and rather tiresome prophets. The scenes at the babe's crib when the offerings are made of the shepherds' pipe, old hat, and mittens, are both droll and tender.

The tragic counterparts of these scenes are those where the Three Executioners work their pitiless task to an end at the Crucifixion, or where the Three Maries go to the grave afterwards in the Cornish mystery, or where Isaac bids his father bind his eyes that he shall not see the sword. It was for long the fashion to say, as Sir Walter Scott did, that these plays had little poetic life, or human interest in them. But they are, at their best, truly touched with essential emotions, with humour, terror, sorrow, pity, as the case may be. Dramatically they are far more alive at this moment, than the English drama of the mid-nineteenth century.

In the Cornish mysteries we lose much by having to use a translation. But something of the spirit and life survive in spite of it, and one detached passage from another of the plays, that of the Crucifixion, is printed in the appendix, which loses nothing by being compared with the treatment in other miracle-plays. Also in the Appendix will be found an interesting note from Norris's Ancient Cornish Drama, on the mode in which the Cornish mysteries were played; and a brief account by Mr. Jenner of the trilogy contained in that work.

There remains John Bayle's play of God's Promises. Its author was born at the sea-doomed city of Dunwich in Suffolk, in 1495. Destined for the church, he showed his obstinacy early by marrying in defiance of his cloth. He was lucky and unlucky in being a protégé of Thomas Cromwell, and had to fly the country on that dangerous agent's death. He returned when the new order was established, and became Bishop of Ossory, had to suffer and turn exile for his tenets again in Mary's reign; but found safe harbourage for his latter years at Canterbury, where he died. He wrote, on his own evidence, more than twenty plays, of which God's Promises, the Life of John the Baptist, and King John, a history play of interest as a pioneer, are best known. He himself called God's Promises a tragedy, but unless the sense of Sodom hanging in the balance, while Abraham works down to its lowest point the diminishing ratio of the just to be found there, or of David's appearing before the Pater Cœlestis as the great judge, of dramatic or tragic emotion there is little indeed. But Bayle's rhetoric easily ran to the edge of suspense, as in the opening of his seventh act, where he puts the dramatic question in the last line:—

I have with fearcenesse mankynde oft tymes corrected,
And agayne I have allured hym by swete promes.
I have sent sore plages, when he hath me neglected,
And then by and by, most confortable swetnes.
To wynne hym to grace, bothe mercye and ryghteousnes
I have exercysed, yet wyll he not amende.
Shall I now lose hym, or shall I hym defende?

And what could be finer than the setting he gives to the antiphon, O Oriens Splendor, at the end of the second act?

To turn from Bayle's play to the heart-breaking realities of Everyman is like turning from a volume of all too edifying sermons to the last chapters of one of the gospels. Into the full history of this play, opening a difficult question about the early relations between Dutch and English writers and printers, there is no room here to go. The Dutch Everyman—Elckerlijk—was in all probability the original of the English, and it was certainly printed a few years earlier. Richard Pynson, who first imprinted the English play at the Sign of the George in Fleet Street, was printing at his press there from the early years of the sixteenth century. The play itself may have been written, and first performed, in English, as in Dutch, a generation or more before.

It was written, no doubt, like most of the plays in this volume, by a churchman; and he must have been a man of profound imagination, and of the tenderest human soul conceivable. His ecclesiastical habit becomes clear enough before the end of the play, where he bids Everyman go and confess his sins. Like many of the more poignant scenes and passages in the miracle-plays that follow it, this morality too leaves one exclaiming on how good a thing was the plain English of the fourteenth and fifteenth centuries.

The relation of the several miracle-plays here printed to the town-cycles from which they come will be seen at a glance on reference to the tables of pageants that appear in the Appendix. We may take it that all these town and country plays represent continually used and frequently tinkered texts, that must in some cases have passed through many piecemeal changes. In making them easy to the average reader of to-day, who takes the place of the mediæval playgoer at a Corpus Christi festival, their latest copyists have but followed in the wake of a series of Tudor scribes who renewed the prompt-books from time to time. In this process, apart from the change of spelling, the smallest possible alteration has been made consistent with the bringing of the text to a fair modern level of intelligibility. Old words that have been familiarised in Malory or Shakespeare, or the Bible, or in the Border Ballads and north-country books, or in Walter Scott, or the modern dialect of Yorkshire, are usually allowed to stand, and words needed to keep the rhyme, are left intact. But really hard words, likely to delay the reader, are glossed. One Towneley play, the Extractio Animarum, another and a most spirited example of the "Harrowing of Hell," mysteries that thrilled the people long ago, is given in the original spelling, as some test of the change effected in the others. Further, in the Appendix will be found a late example of a St. George and the Dragon doggerel Christmas play, which comes from Cornwall, and which in a slightly varying form has been played in many shires, from Wessex to Tyneside, within living memory. This shows us the last state of the traditional mystery, and the English folk-play as it became when it was left to the village wits and playwrights to produce it, without any co-operation from the trained eye and hand of a parson or a learned clerk. Of some other forms of our earlier drama, not omitting the Welsh interludes of Twm o'r Nant, it may be possible to give illustrations in a later book, companion to this. Only so much is given here as may interest the reader, who is a playgoer first of all, and asks for entertainment and a light in these darker passages of the old British drama.

Finally the amplest acknowledgments are due to those who have worked upon these present plays, including Mrs. C. Richardson, M.A., Mr. O'Brien, Mr. Roberts, Miss Hawkins, G. R., and Mr. Ezra Pound; and to the various editors of the "Early English Text Society," who have made this book possible. Especially should tribute be paid to Dr. Furnivall for his permission to make use of the Society's texts, and his interest in this uncertain attempt to capture the outer public too, and attract it to that ever-living literature to which he has devoted so many days of his young old-age.

E. R.

Everyman: a moral play otherwise called: A Treatyse how the hye fader of heven sendeth dethe to somon every creature to come and gyve a counte of theyr lyves in this worlde] , translated from the Dutch play, Elckerlijk, 1520 (?); published in Dodsley's Select Collection of Old English Plays, etc., vol. I., 1874; reprint of one of Skot's editions, collated with his other edition and those of Pynson, Ed. H. Logeman, 1892; with an introduction by F. Sidgwick, 1902; reprinted by W. W. Greg from the Edition by John Skot preserved at Britwell Court, 1904; set to music by H. Walford Davies, etc. (with historical and analytical notes), 1904; J. S. Farmer, Six Anonymous Plays (Early English Dramatists), 1905; with designs by Ambrose Dudley, 1906; in Broadway Booklets, 1906; with introduction, note-book, and word list, J. S. Farmer (Museum Dramatists), 1906.

Miracle Plays: Towneley Mysteries, ed. by Surtees Society, 1836; Pollard, Early English Text Society, 1897. York Mysteries, ed. Lucy

Toulmin Smith, 1885. Chester Mysteries, ed. Th. Wright, Shakespeare Society, 1843-47; Deimling, Early English Text Society, 1893, etc.; T. H. Markland (two plays), Roxburghe Club, 1818. Coventry Mysteries, ed. Halliwell, Shakespeare Society, 1841. See also Sharp, Dissertation on the Coventry Mysteries. For other Mysteries see Davidson, Modern Language Notes, vii.; E. Norris, Ancient Cornish Drama, 1859.

Selections, or Separate Plays: Harrowing of Hell, ed. Halliwell, 1840; Collier, Five Miracle Plays, 1867; Dr. E. Mall, 1871; A. W. Pollard, English Miracle Plays, 1895; Specimens of the Pre-Shakespearean Drama, 1897, 2 vols. (a third vol. to come), Prof. Manly. See J. H. Kirkham (Enquiry into Sources, etc.), 1885. Abraham and Isaac, ed. L. Toulmin Smith (Brome Hall MS.), 1886; R. Brotanek (Dublin MS.), Anglia, xxi.

General Literature: Ward, History of English Dramatic Literature, 1875-6; Payne Collier, The History of English Dramatic Poetry, 1879; K. Hase, Miracle Plays, trans. A. W. Jackson, 1880; C. Davidson, Studies in English Mystery Plays, 1892; A. W. Pollard, English Miracle Plays, Moralities, and Interludes, Specimens of pre-Elizabethan Drama, etc., 1895; K. Chambers, The Mediæval Stage, 1903; A full bibliography is given in F. H. Stoddard, References for Students of Miracle Plays and Mysteries, 1887.

Everyman

CHARACTERS

EVERYMAN
GOD: ADONAI
DEATH
MESSENGER
FELLOWSHIP
COUSIN
KINDRED
GOODS
GOOD-DEEDS
STRENGTH
DISCRETION
FIVE-WITS
BEAUTY
KNOWLEDGE
CONFESSION
ANGEL
DOCTOR

EVERYMAN

HERE BEGINNETH A TREATISE HOW THE HIGH FATHER OF
HEAVEN SENDETH DEATH TO SUMMON EVERY CREATURE
TO COME AND GIVE ACCOUNT OF THEIR LIVES IN THIS
WORLD AND IS IN MANNER OF A MORAL PLAY.

MESSENGER. I pray you all give your audience,
     And hear this matter with reverence,
     By figure a moral play—
     The Summoning of Everyman called it is,
     That of our lives and ending shows
     How transitory we be all day.
     This matter is wondrous precious,
     But the intent of it is more gracious,
     And sweet to bear away.
     The story saith,—Man, in the beginning,
     Look well, and take good heed to the ending,
     Be you never so gay!
     Ye think sin in the beginning full sweet,
     Which in the end causeth thy soul to weep,
     When the body lieth in clay.

Here shall you see how Fellowship and Jollity,
Both Strength, Pleasure, and Beauty,
Will fade from thee as flower in May.
For ye shall hear, how our heaven king
Calleth Everyman to a general reckoning:
Give audience, and hear what he doth say.

GOD. I perceive here in my majesty,
How that all creatures be to me unkind,
Living without dread in worldly prosperity:
Of ghostly sight the people be so blind,
Drowned in sin, they know me not for their God;
In worldly riches is all their mind,
They fear not my rightwiseness, the sharp rod;
My law that I shewed, when I for them died,
They forget clean, and shedding of my blood red;
I hanged between two, it cannot be denied;
To get them life I suffered to be dead;
I healed their feet, with thorns hurt was my head:
I could do no more than I did truly,
And now I see the people do clean forsake me.
They use the seven deadly sins damnable;
As pride, covetise, wrath, and lechery,
Now in the world be made commendable;
And thus they leave of angels the heavenly company;
Everyman liveth so after his own pleasure,
And yet of their life they be nothing sure:
I see the more that I them forbear
The worse they be from year to year;
All that liveth appaireth⁷ fast,
Therefore I will in all the haste
Have a reckoning of Everyman's person
For and I leave the people thus alone
In their life and wicked tempests,
Verily they will become much worse than beasts;
For now one would by envy another up eat;
Charity they all do clean forget.
I hoped well that Everyman
In my glory should make his mansion,
And thereto I had them all elect;
But now I see, like traitors deject,
They thank me not for the pleasure that I to them meant,
Nor yet for their being that I them have lent;
I proffered the people great multitude of mercy,

---

⁷ is impaired.

And few there be that asketh it heartily;
They be so cumbered with worldly riches,
That needs on them I must do justice,
On Everyman living without fear.
Where art thou, Death, thou mighty messenger?

DEATH. Almighty God, I am here at your will,
Your commandment to fulfil.

GOD. Go thou to Everyman,
And show him in my name
A pilgrimage he must on him take,
Which he in no wise may escape;
And that he bring with him a sure reckoning
Without delay or any tarrying.

DEATH. Lord, I will in the world go run over all,
And cruelly outsearch both great and small;
Every man will I beset that liveth beastly
Out of God's laws, and dreadeth not folly:
He that loveth riches I will strike with my dart,
His sight to blind, and from heaven to depart,
Except that alms be his good friend,
In hell for to dwell, world without end.
Lo, yonder I see Everyman walking;
Full little he thinketh on my coming;
His mind is on fleshly lusts and his treasure,
And great pain it shall cause him to endure
Before the Lord Heaven King.
Everyman, stand still; whither art thou going
Thus gaily? Hast thou thy Maker forget?

EVERYMAN. Why askst thou?
Wouldest thou wete?[8]

DEATH. Yea, sir, I will show you;
In great haste I am sent to thee
From God out of his majesty.

EVERYMAN. What, sent to me?

DEATH. Yea, certainly.
Though thou have forget him here,
He thinketh on thee in the heavenly sphere,
As, or we depart, thou shalt know.

EVERYMAN. What desireth God of me?

DEATH. That shall I show thee;
A reckoning he will needs have
Without any longer respite.

EVERYMAN. To give a reckoning longer leisure I crave;

---

[8] know.

This blind matter troubleth my wit. S T O P

STOP DEATH. On thee thou must take a long journey:
    Therefore thy book of count with thee thou bring;
    For turn again thou can not by no way,
    And look thou be sure of thy reckoning:
    For before God thou shalt answer, and show
    Thy many bad deeds and good but a few;
    How thou hast spent thy life, and in what wise,
    Before the chief lord of paradise.
    Have ado that we were in that way,
    For, wete thou well, thou shalt make none attournay.[9]

EVERYMAN. Full unready I am such reckoning to give.
    I know thee not: what messenger art thou?

DEATH. I am Death, that no man dreadeth.
    For every man I rest and no man spareth;
    For it is God's commandment
    That all to me should be obedient.

EVERYMAN. O Death, thou comest when I had thee least in mind;
    In thy power it lieth me to save,
    Yet of my good will I give thee, if ye will be kind,
    Yea, a thousand pound shalt thou have,
    And defer this matter till another day.

DEATH. Everyman, it may not be by no way;
    I set not by gold, silver, nor riches,
    Ne by pope, emperor, king, duke, ne princes.
    For and I would receive gifts great,
    All the world I might get;
    But my custom is clean contrary.
    I give thee no respite: come hence, and not tarry.

EVERYMAN. Alas, shall I have no longer respite?
    I may say Death giveth no warning:
    To think on thee, it maketh my heart sick,
    For all unready is my book of reckoning.
    But twelve year and I might have abiding,
    My counting book I would make so clear,
    That my reckoning I should not need to fear.
    Wherefore, Death, I pray thee, for God's mercy,
    Spare me till I be provided of remedy.

DEATH. Thee availeth not to cry, weep, and pray:
    But haste thee lightly that you were gone the journey,
    And prove thy friends if thou can.
    For, wete thou well, the tide abideth no man,
    And in the world each living creature

---

[9] mediator.

For Adam's sin must die of nature.

EVERYMAN. Death, if I should this pilgrimage take,
 And my reckoning surely make,
 Show me, for saint charity,
 Should I not come again shortly?

DEATH. No, Everyman; and thou be once there,
 Thou mayst never more come here,
 Trust me verily.

EVERYMAN. O gracious God, in the high seat celestial,
 Have mercy on me in this most need;
 Shall I have no company from this vale terrestrial
 Of mine acquaintance that way me to lead?

DEATH. Yea, if any be so hardy,
 That would go with thee and bear thee company.
 Hie thee that you were gone to God's magnificence,
 Thy reckoning to give before his presence.
 What, weenest thou thy life is given thee,
 And thy worldly goods also?

EVERYMAN. I had wend so, verily.

DEATH. Nay, nay; it was but lent thee;
 For as soon as thou art go,
 Another awhile shall have it, and then go therefro
 Even as thou hast done.
 Everyman, thou art mad; thou hast thy wits five,
 And here on earth will not amend thy life,
 For suddenly I do come.

EVERYMAN. O wretched caitiff, whither shall I flee,
 That I might scape this endless sorrow!
 Now, gentle Death, spare me till to-morrow,
 That I may amend me
 With good advisement.

DEATH. Nay, thereto I will not consent,
 Nor no man will I respite,
 But to the heart suddenly I shall smite
 Without any advisement.
 And now out of thy sight I will me hie;
 See thou make thee ready shortly,
 For thou mayst say this is the day
 That no man living may scape away.

EVERYMAN. Alas, I may well weep with sighs deep;
 Now have I no manner of company
 To help me in my journey, and me to keep;
 And also my writing is full unready.
 How shall I do now for to excuse me?

I would to God I had never be gete![10]
To my soul a full great profit it had be;
For now I fear pains huge and great.
The time passeth; Lord, help that all wrought;
For though I mourn it availeth nought.
The day passeth, and is almost a-go;
I wot not well what for to do.
To whom were I best my complaint to make?
What, and I to Fellowship thereof spake,
And showed him of this sudden chance?
For in him is all mine affiance;
We have in the world so many a day
Be on good friends in sport and play.
I see him yonder, certainly;
I trust that he will bear me company;
Therefore to him will I speak to ease my sorrow.
Well met, good Fellowship, and good morrow!
FELLOWSHIP. Everyman, good morrow by this day.
   Sir, why lookest thou so piteously?
   If any thing be amiss, I pray thee, me say,
   That I may help to remedy.
EVERYMAN. Yea, good Fellowship, yea,
   I am in great jeopardy.
FELLOWSHIP. My true friend, show to me your mind;
   I will not forsake thee, unto my life's end,
   In the way of good company.
EVERYMAN. That was well spoken, and lovingly.
FELLOWSHIP. Sir, I must needs know your heaviness;
   I have pity to see you in any distress;
   If any have you wronged ye shall revenged be,
   Though I on the ground be slain for thee,—
   Though that I know before that I should die.
EVERYMAN. Verily, Fellowship, gramercy.
FELLOWSHIP. Tush! by thy thanks I set not a straw.
   Show me your grief, and say no more.
EVERYMAN. If I my heart should to you break,
   And then you to turn your mind from me,
   And would not me comfort, when you hear me speak,
   Then should I ten times sorrier be.
FELLOWSHIP. Sir, I say as I will do in deed.
EVERYMAN. Then be you a good friend at need:
   I have found you true here before.
FELLOWSHIP. And so ye shall evermore;

---

[10] been gotten, been born.

> For, in faith, and thou go to Hell,
> I will not forsake thee by the way!

EVERYMAN. Ye speak like a good friend; I believe you well;
> I shall deserve it, and I may.

FELLOWSHIP. I speak of no deserving, by this day.
> For he that will say and nothing do
> Is not worthy with good company to go;
> Therefore show me the grief of your mind,
> As to your friend most loving and kind.

EVERYMAN. I shall show you how it is;
> Commanded I am to go a journey,
> A long way, hard and dangerous,
> And give a strait count without delay
> Before the high judge Adonai.[11]
> Wherefore I pray you, bear me company,
> As ye have promised, in this journey.

FELLOWSHIP. That is matter indeed! Promise is duty,
> But, and I should take such a voyage on me,
> I know it well, it should be to my pain:
> Also it make me afeard, certain.
> But let us take counsel here as well as we can,
> For your words would fear a strong man.

EVERYMAN. Why, ye said, If I had need,
> Ye would me never forsake, quick nor dead,
> Though it were to hell truly.

FELLOWSHIP. So I said, certainly,
> But such pleasures be set aside, thee sooth to say:
> And also, if we took such a journey,
> When should we come again?

EVERYMAN. Nay, never again till the day of doom.

FELLOWSHIP. In faith, then will not I come there!
> Who hath you these tidings brought?

EVERYMAN. Indeed, Death was with me here.

FELLOWSHIP. Now, by God that all hath bought,
> If Death were the messenger,
> For no man that is living to-day
> I will not go that loath journey—
> Not for the father that begat me!

EVERYMAN. Ye promised other wise, pardie.

FELLOWSHIP. I wot well I say so truly;
> And yet if thou wilt eat, and drink, and make good cheer,
> Or haunt to women, the lusty company,
> I would not forsake you, while the day is clear,

---

[11] God.

Trust me verily!

EVERYMAN. Yea, thereto ye would be ready;
 To go to mirth, solace, and play,
 Your mind will sooner apply
 Than to bear me company in my long journey.

FELLOWSHIP. Now, in good faith, I will not that way.
 But and thou wilt murder, or any man kill,
 In that I will help thee with a good will!

EVERYMAN. O that is a simple advice indeed!
 Gentle fellow, help me in my necessity;
 We have loved long, and now I need,
 And now, gentle Fellowship, remember me.

FELLOWSHIP. Whether ye have loved me or no,
 By Saint John, I will not with thee go.

EVERYMAN. Yet I pray thee, take the labour, and do so much for me
 To bring me forward, for saint charity,
 And comfort me till I come without the town.

FELLOWSHIP. Nay, and thou would give me a new gown,
 I will not a foot with thee go;
 But and you had tarried I would not have left thee so.
 And as now, God speed thee in thy journey,
 For from thee I will depart as fast as I may.

EVERYMAN. Whither away, Fellowship? will you forsake me?

FELLOWSHIP. Yea, by my fay, to God I betake thee.

EVERYMAN. Farewell, good Fellowship; for this my heart is sore;
 Adieu for ever, I shall see thee no more.

FELLOWSHIP. In faith, Everyman, farewell now at the end;
 For you I will remember that parting is mourning.

EVERYMAN. Alack! shall we thus depart indeed?
 Our Lady, help, without any more comfort,
 Lo, Fellowship forsaketh me in my most need:
 For help in this world whither shall I resort?
 Fellowship herebefore with me would merry make;
 And now little sorrow for me doth he take.
 It is said, in prosperity men friends may find,
 Which in adversity be full unkind.
 Now whither for succour shall I flee,
 Sith that Fellowship hath forsaken me?
 To my kinsmen I will truly,
 Praying them to help me in my necessity;
 I believe that they will do so,
 For kind will creep where it may not go.
 I will go say, for yonder I see them go.
 Where be ye now, my friends and kinsmen?

KINDRED. Here be we now at your commandment.

Cousin, I pray you show us your intent
In any wise, and not spare.

COUSIN. Yea, Everyman, and to us declare
If ye be disposed to go any whither,
For wete you well, we will live and die together.

KINDRED. In wealth and woe we will with you hold,
For over his kin a man may be bold.

EVERYMAN. Gramercy, my friends and kinsmen kind.
Now shall I show you the grief of my mind:
I was commanded by a messenger,
That is an high king's chief officer;
He bade me go a pilgrimage to my pain,
And I know well I shall never come again;
Also I must give a reckoning straight,
For I have a great enemy, that hath me in wait,
Which intendeth me for to hinder.

KINDRED. What account is that which ye must render?
That would I know.

EVERYMAN. Of all my works I must show
How I have lived and my days spent;
Also of ill deeds, that I have used
In my time, sith life was me lent;
And of all virtues that I have refused.
Therefore I pray you go thither with me,
To help to make mine account, for saint charity.

COUSIN. What, to go thither? Is that the matter?
Nay, Everyman, I had liefer fast bread and water
All this five year and more.

EVERYMAN. Alas, that ever I was bore![12]
For now shall I never be merry
If that you forsake me.

KINDRED. Ah, sir; what, ye be a merry man!
Take good heart to you, and make no moan.
But one thing I warn you, by Saint Anne,
As for me, ye shall go alone.

EVERYMAN. My Cousin, will you not with me go?

COUSIN. No, by our Lady; I have the cramp in my toe.
Trust not to me, for, so God me speed,
I will deceive you in your most need,

KINDRED. It availeth not us to tice.
Ye shall have my maid with all my heart;
She loveth to go to feasts, there to be nice,
And to dance, and abroad to start:

---

[12] born.

I will give her leave to help you in that journey,
If that you and she may agree.
EVERYMAN. Now show me the very effect of your mind.
Will you go with me, or abide behind?
KINDRED. Abide behind? yea, that I will and I may!
Therefore farewell until another day.
EVERYMAN. How should I be merry or glad?
For fair promises to me make,
But when I have most need, they me forsake.
I am deceived; that maketh me sad.
COUSIN. Cousin Everyman, farewell now,
For verily I will not go with you;
Also of mine own an unready reckoning
I have to account; therefore I make tarrying.
Now, God keep thee, for now I go.
EVERYMAN. Ah, Jesus, is all come hereto?
Lo, fair words maketh fools feign;
They promise and nothing will do certain.
My kinsmen promised me faithfully
For to abide with me steadfastly,
And now fast away do they flee:
Even so Fellowship promised me.
What friend were best me of to provide?
I lose my time here longer to abide.
Yet in my mind a thing there is;—
All my life I have loved riches;
If that my good now help me might,
He would make my heart full light.
I will speak to him in this distress.—
Where art thou, my Goods and riches?
GOODS. Who calleth me? Everyman? what haste thou hast!
I lie here in corners, trussed and piled so high,
And in chests I am locked so fast,
Also sacked in bags, thou mayst see with thine eye,
I cannot stir; in packs low I lie.
What would ye have, lightly me say.
EVERYMAN. Come hither, Good, in all the haste thou may,
For of counsel I must desire thee.
GOODS. Sir, and ye in the world have trouble or adversity,
That can I help you to remedy shortly.
EVERYMAN. It is another disease that grieveth me;
In this world it is not, I tell thee so.
I am sent for another way to go,
To give a straight account general
Before the highest Jupiter of all;

And all my life I have had joy and pleasure in thee.
Therefore I pray thee go with me,
For, peradventure, thou mayst before God Almighty
My reckoning help to clean and purify;
For it is said ever among,
That money maketh all right that is wrong.

GOODS. Nay, Everyman, I sing another song,
I follow no man in such voyages;
For and I went with thee
Thou shouldst fare much the worse for me;
For because on me thou did set thy mind,
Thy reckoning I have made blotted and blind,
That thine account thou cannot make truly;
And that hast thou for the love of me.

EVERYMAN. That would grieve me full sore,
When I should come to that fearful answer.
Up, let us go thither together.

GOODS. Nay, not so, I am too brittle, I may not endure;
I will follow no man one foot, be ye sure.

EVERYMAN. Alas, I have thee loved, and had great pleasure
All my life-days on good and treasure.

GOODS. That is to thy damnation without lesing,
For my love is contrary to the love everlasting.
But if thou had me loved moderately during,
As, to the poor give part of me,
Then shouldst thou not in this dolour be,
Nor in this great sorrow and care.

EVERYMAN. Lo, now was I deceived or I was ware,
And all I may wyte[13] my spending of time.

GOODS. What, weenest thou that I am thine?

EVERYMAN. I had wend so.

GOODS. Nay, Everyman, I say no;
As for a while I was lent thee,
A season thou hast had me in prosperity;
My condition is man's soul to kill;
If I save one, a thousand I do spill;
Weenest thou that I will follow thee?
Nay, from this world, not verily.

EVERYMAN. I had wend otherwise.

GOODS. Therefore to thy soul Good is a thief;
For when thou art dead, this is my guise
Another to deceive in the same wise
As I have done thee, and all to his soul's reprief.

---

[13] blame.

EVERYMAN. O false Good, cursed thou be!
> Thou traitor to God, that hast deceived me,
> And caught me in thy snare.

GOODS. Marry, thou brought thyself in care,
> Whereof I am glad,
> I must needs laugh, I cannot be sad.

EVERYMAN. Ah, Good, thou hast had long my heartly love;
> I gave thee that which should be the Lord's above.
> But wilt thou not go with me in deed?
> I pray thee truth to say.

GOODS. No, so God me speed,
> Therefore farewell, and have good day.

EVERYMAN. O, to whom shall I make my moan
> For to go with me in that heavy journey?
> First Fellowship said he would with me gone;
> His words were very pleasant and gay,
> But afterward he left me alone.
> Then spake I to my kinsmen all in despair,
> And also they gave me words fair,
> They lacked no fair speaking,
> But all forsake me in the ending.
> Then went I to my Goods that I loved best,
> In hope to have comfort, but there had I least;
> For my Goods sharply did me tell
> That he bringeth many into hell.
> Then of myself I was ashamed,
> And so I am worthy to be blamed;
> Thus may I well myself hate.
> Of whom shall I now counsel take?
> I think that I shall never speed
> Till that I go to my Good-Deed,
> But alas, she is so weak,
> That she can neither go nor speak;
> Yet will I venture on her now.—
> My Good-Deeds, where be you?

GOOD-DEEDS. Here I lie cold in the ground;
> Thy sins hath me sore bound,
> That I cannot stir.

EVERYMAN. O, Good-Deeds, I stand in fear;
> I must you pray of counsel,
> For help now should come right well.

GOOD-DEEDS. Everyman, I have understanding
> That ye be summoned account to make
> Before Messias, of Jerusalem King;

And you do by me[14] that journey what[15] you will I take.
EVERYMAN. Therefore I come to you, my moan to make;
    I pray you, that ye will go with me.
GOOD-DEEDS. I would full fain, but I cannot stand verily.
EVERYMAN. Why, is there anything on you fall?
GOOD-DEEDS. Yea, sir, I may thank you of all;
    If ye had perfectly cheered me,
    Your book of account now full ready had be.
    Look, the books of your works and deeds eke;
    Oh, see how they lie under the feet,
    To your soul's heaviness.
EVERYMAN. Our Lord Jesus, help me!
    For one letter here I can not see.
GOOD-DEEDS. There is a blind reckoning in time of distress!
EVERYMAN. Good-Deeds, I pray you, help me in this need,
    Or else I am for ever damned indeed;
    Therefore help me to make reckoning
    Before the redeemer of all thing,
    That king is, and was, and ever shall.
GOOD-DEEDS. Everyman, I am sorry of your fall,
    And fain would I help you, and I were able.
EVERYMAN. Good-Deeds, your counsel I pray you give me.
GOOD-DEEDS. That shall I do verily;
    Though that on my feet I may not go,
    I have a sister, that shall with you also,
    Called Knowledge, which shall with you abide,
    To help you to make that dreadful reckoning.
KNOWLEDGE. Everyman, I will go with thee, and be thy guide,
    In thy most need to go by thy side.
EVERYMAN. In good condition I am now in every thing,
    And am wholly content with this good thing;
    Thanked be God my Creator.
GOOD-DEEDS. And when he hath brought thee there,
    Where thou shalt heal thee of thy smart,
    Then go you with your reckoning and your Good-Deeds together
    For to make you joyful at heart
    Before the blessed Trinity.
EVERYMAN. My Good-Deeds, gramercy;
    I am well content, certainly,
    With your words sweet.
KNOWLEDGE. Now go we together lovingly,
    To Confession, that cleansing river.

---

[14] If you go by me.
[15] with.

EVERYMAN. For joy I weep; I would we were there;
    But, I pray you, give me cognition
    Where dwelleth that holy man, Confession.
KNOWLEDGE. In the house of salvation:
    We shall find him in that place,
    That shall us comfort by God's grace.
    Lo, this is Confession; kneel down and ask mercy,
    For he is in good conceit with God almighty.
EVERYMAN. O glorious fountain that all uncleanness doth clarify,
    Wash from me the spots of vices unclean,
    That on me no sin may be seen;
    I come with Knowledge for my redemption,
    Repent with hearty and full contrition;
    For I am commanded a pilgrimage to take,
    And great accounts before God to make.
    Now, I pray you, Shrift, mother of salvation,
    Help my good deeds for my piteous exclamation.
CONFESSION. I know your sorrow well, Everyman;
    Because with Knowledge ye come to me,
    I will you comfort as well as I can,
    And a precious jewel I will give thee,
    Called penance, wise voider of adversity;
    Therewith shall your body chastised be,
    With abstinence and perseverance in God's service:
    Here shall you receive that scourge of me,
    Which is penance strong, that ye must endure,
    To remember thy Saviour was scourged for thee
    With sharp scourges, and suffered it patiently;
    So must thou, or thou scape that painful pilgrimage;
    Knowledge, keep him in this voyage,
    And by that time Good-Deeds will be with thee.
    But in any wise, be sure of mercy,
    For your time draweth fast, and ye will saved be;
    Ask God mercy, and He will grant truly,
    When with the scourge of penance man doth him bind,
    The oil of forgiveness then shall he find.
EVERYMAN. Thanked be God for his gracious work!
    For now I will my penance begin;
    This hath rejoiced and lighted my heart,
    Though the knots be painful and hard within.
KNOWLEDGE. Everyman, look your penance that ye fulfil,
    What pain that ever it to you be,
    And Knowledge shall give you counsel at will,
    How your accounts ye shall make clearly.
EVERYMAN. O eternal God, O heavenly figure,

O way of rightwiseness, O goodly vision,
Which descended down in a virgin pure
Because he would Everyman redeem,
Which Adam forfeited by his disobedience:
O blessed Godhead, elect and high-divine,
Forgive my grievous offence;
Here I cry thee mercy in this presence.
O ghostly treasure, O ransomer and redeemer
Of all the world, hope and conductor,
Mirror of joy, and founder of mercy,
Which illumineth heaven and earth thereby,
Hear my clamorous complaint, though it late be;
Receive my prayers; unworthy in this heavy life,
Though I be, a sinner most abominable,
Yet let my name be written in Moses' table;
O Mary, pray to the Maker of all thing,
Me for to help at my ending,
And save me from the power of my enemy,
For Death assaileth me strongly;
And, Lady, that I may by means of thy prayer
Of your Son's glory to be partaker,
By the means of his passion I it crave,
I beseech you, help my soul to save.—
Knowledge, give me the scourge of penance;
My flesh therewith shall give a quittance:
I will now begin, if God give me grace.

KNOWLEDGE. Everyman, God give you time and space:
Thus I bequeath you in the hands of our Saviour,
Thus may you make your reckoning sure.

EVERYMAN. In the name of the Holy Trinity,
My body sore punished shall be:
Take this body for the sin of the flesh;
Also thou delightest to go gay and fresh,
And in the way of damnation thou did me bring;
Therefore suffer now strokes and punishing.
Now of penance I will wade the water clear,
To save me from purgatory, that sharp fire.

GOOD-DEEDS. I thank God, now I can walk and go;
And am delivered of my sickness and woe.
Therefore with Everyman I will go, and not spare;
His good works I will help him to declare.

KNOWLEDGE. Now, Everyman, be merry and glad;
Your Good-Deeds cometh now; ye may not be sad;
Now is your Good-Deeds whole and sound,
Going upright upon the ground.

EVERYMAN. My heart is light, and shall be evermore;
    Now will I smite faster than I did before.
GOOD-DEEDS. Everyman, pilgrim, my special friend,
    Blessed be thou without end;
    For thee is prepared the eternal glory.
    Ye have me made whole and sound,
    Therefore I will bide by thee in every stound.[16]
EVERYMAN. Welcome, my Good-Deeds; now I hear thy voice,
    I weep for very sweetness of love.
KNOWLEDGE. Be no more sad, but ever rejoice,
    God seeth thy living in his throne above;
    Put on this garment to thy behove,
    Which is wet with your tears,
    Or else before God you may it miss,
    When you to your journey's end come shall.
EVERYMAN. Gentle Knowledge, what do you it call?
KNOWLEDGE. It is a garment of sorrow:
    From pain it will you borrow;
    Contrition it is,
    That getteth forgiveness;
    It pleaseth God passing well.
GOOD-DEEDS. Everyman, will you wear it for your heal?
EVERYMAN. Now blessed be Jesu, Mary's Son!
    For now have I on true contrition.
    And let us go now without tarrying;
    Good-Deeds, have we clear our reckoning?
GOOD-DEEDS. Yea, indeed I have it here.
EVERYMAN. Then I trust we need not fear;
    Now, friends, let us not part in twain.
KNOWLEDGE. Nay, Everyman, that will we not, certain.
GOOD-DEEDS. Yet must thou lead with thee
    Three persons of great might.
EVERYMAN. Who should they be?
GOOD-DEEDS. Discretion and Strength they hight,
    And thy Beauty may not abide behind.
KNOWLEDGE. Also ye must call to mind
    Your Five-wits as for your counsellors.
GOOD-DEEDS. You must have them ready at all hours.
EVERYMAN. How shall I get them hither?
KNOWLEDGE. You must call them all together,
    And they will hear you incontinent.
EVERYMAN. My friends, come hither and be present
    Discretion, Strength, my Five-wits, and Beauty.

---

[16] season.

BEAUTY. Here at your will we be all ready.
    What will ye that we should do?
GOOD-DEEDS. That ye would with Everyman go,
    And help him in his pilgrimage,
    Advise you, will ye with him or not in that voyage?
STRENGTH. We will bring him all thither,
    To his help and comfort, ye may believe me.
DISCRETION. So will we go with him all together.
EVERYMAN. Almighty God, loved thou be,
    I give thee laud that I have hither brought
    Strength, Discretion, Beauty, and Five-wits; lack I nought;
    And my Good-Deeds, with Knowledge clear,
    All be in my company at my will here;
    I desire no more to my business.
STRENGTH. And I, Strength, will by you stand in distress,
    Though thou would in battle fight on the ground.
FIVE-WITS. And though it were through the world round,
    We will not depart for sweet nor sour.
BEAUTY. No more will I unto death's hour,
    Whatsoever thereof befall.
DISCRETION. Everyman, advise you first of all;
    Go with a good advisement and deliberation;
    We all give you virtuous monition
    That all shall be well.
EVERYMAN. My friends, hearken what I will tell:
    I pray God reward you in his heavenly sphere.
    Now hearken, all that be here,
    For I will make my testament
    Here before you all present.
    In alms half my good I will give with my hands twain
    In the way of charity, with good intent,
    And the other half still shall remain
    In quiet to be returned there it ought to be.
    This I do in despite of the fiend of hell
    To go quite out of his peril
    Ever after and this day.
KNOWLEDGE. Everyman, hearken what I say;
    Go to priesthood, I you advise,
    And receive of him in any wise
    The holy sacrament and ointment together;
    Then shortly see ye turn again hither;
    We will all abide you here.
FIVE-WITS. Yea, Everyman, hie you that ye ready were,
    There is no emperor, king, duke, ne baron,
    That of God hath commission,

As hath the least priest in the world being;
For of the blessed sacraments pure and benign,
He beareth the keys and thereof hath the cure
For man's redemption, it is ever sure;
Which God for our soul's medicine
Gave us out of his heart with great pine;
Here in this transitory life, for thee and me
The blessed sacraments seven there be,
Baptism, confirmation, with priesthood good,
And the sacrament of God's precious flesh and blood,
Marriage, the holy extreme unction, and penance;
These seven be good to have in remembrance,
Gracious sacraments of high divinity.

EVERYMAN. Fain would I receive that holy body
And meekly to my ghostly father I will go.

FIVE-WITS. Everyman, that is the best that ye can do:
God will you to salvation bring,
For priesthood exceedeth all other thing;
To us Holy Scripture they do teach,
And converteth man from sin heaven to reach;
God hath to them more power given,
Than to any angel that is in heaven;
With five words he may consecrate
God's body in flesh and blood to make,
And handleth his maker between his hands;
The priest bindeth and unbindeth all bands,
Both in earth and in heaven;
Thou ministers all the sacraments seven;
Though we kissed thy feet thou were worthy;
Thou art surgeon that cureth sin deadly:
No remedy we find under God
But all only priesthood.
Everyman, God gave priests that dignity,
And setteth them in his stead among us to be;
Thus be they above angels in degree.

KNOWLEDGE. If priests be good it is so surely;
But when Jesus hanged on the cross with great smart
There he gave, out of his blessed heart,
The same sacrament in great torment:
He sold them not to us, that Lord Omnipotent.
Therefore Saint Peter the apostle doth say
That Jesu's curse hath all they
Which God their Saviour do buy or sell,
Or they for any money do take or tell.
Sinful priests giveth the sinners example bad;

Their children sitteth by other men's fires, I have heard;
And some haunteth women's company,
With unclean life, as lusts of lechery
These be with sin made blind. STOP

START FIVE-WITS. I trust to God no such may we find;
Therefore let us priesthood honour,
And follow their doctrine for our souls' succour;
We be their sheep, and they shepherds be
By whom we all be kept in surety.
Peace, for yonder I see Everyman come,
Which hath made true satisfaction.
GOOD-DEEDS. Methinketh it is he indeed.
EVERYMAN. Now Jesu be our alder speed.[17]
I have received the sacrament for my redemption,
And then mine extreme unction:
Blessed be all they that counselled me to take it!
And now, friends, let us go without longer respite;
I thank God that ye have tarried so long.
Now set each of you on this rod your hand,
And shortly follow me:
I go before, there I would be; God be our guide.
STRENGTH. Everyman, we will not from you go,
Till ye have gone this voyage long.
DISCRETION. I, Discretion, will bide by you also.
KNOWLEDGE. And though this pilgrimage be never so strong,
I will never part you fro:
Everyman, I will be as sure by thee
As ever I did by Judas Maccabee.
EVERYMAN. Alas, I am so faint I may not stand,
My limbs under me do fold;
Friends, let us not turn again to this land,
Not for all the world's gold,
For into this cave must I creep
And turn to the earth and there to sleep.
BEAUTY. What, into this grave? alas!
EVERYMAN. Yea, there shall you consume more and less.
BEAUTY. And what, should I smother here?
EVERYMAN. Yea, by my faith, and never more appear.
In this world live no more we shall,
But in heaven before the highest Lord of all.
BEAUTY. I cross out all this; adieu by Saint John;
I take my cap in my lap and am gone.
EVERYMAN. What, Beauty, whither will ye?

---

[17] speed in help of all.

BEAUTY. Peace, I am deaf; I look not behind me,
    Not and thou would give me all the gold in thy chest.
EVERYMAN. Alas, whereto may I trust?
    Beauty goeth fast away hie;
    She promised with me to live and die.
STRENGTH. Everyman, I will thee also forsake and deny;
    Thy game liketh me not at all.
EVERYMAN. Why, then ye will forsake me all.
    Sweet Strength, tarry a little space.
STRENGTH. Nay, sir, by the rood of grace
    I will hie me from thee fast,
    Though thou weep till thy heart brast.
EVERYMAN. Ye would ever bide by me, ye said.
STRENGTH. Yea, I have you far enough conveyed;
    Ye be old enough, I understand,
    Your pilgrimage to take on hand;
    I repent me that I hither came.
EVERYMAN. Strength, you to displease I am to blame;
    Will you break promise that is debt?
STRENGTH. In faith, I care not;
    Thou art but a fool to complain,
    You spend your speech and waste your brain;
    Go thrust thee into the ground.
EVERYMAN. I had wend surer I should you have found.
    He that trusteth in his Strength
    She him deceiveth at the length.
    Both Strength and Beauty forsaketh me,
    Yet they promised me fair and lovingly.
DISCRETION. Everyman, I will after Strength be gone,
    As for me I will leave you alone.
EVERYMAN. Why, Discretion, will ye forsake me?
DISCRETION. Yea, in faith, I will go from thee,
    For when Strength goeth before
    I follow after evermore.
EVERYMAN. Yet, I pray thee, for the love of the Trinity,
    Look in my grave once piteously.
DISCRETION. Nay, so nigh will I not come.
    Farewell, every one!
EVERYMAN. O all thing faileth, save God alone;
    Beauty, Strength, and Discretion;
    For when Death bloweth his blast,
    They all run from me full fast.
FIVE-WITS. Everyman, my leave now of thee I take;
    I will follow the other, for here I thee forsake.
EVERYMAN. Alas! then may I wail and weep,

For I took you for my best friend.
FIVE-WITS. I will no longer thee keep;
　　Now farewell, and there an end.
EVERYMAN. O Jesu, help, all hath forsaken me!
GOOD-DEEDS. Nay, Everyman, I will bide with thee,
　　I will not forsake thee indeed;
　　Thou shalt find me a good friend at need.
EVERYMAN. Gramercy, Good-Deeds; now may I true friends see;
　　They have forsaken me every one;
　　I loved them better than my Good-Deeds alone.
　　Knowledge, will ye forsake me also?
KNOWLEDGE. Yea, Everyman, when ye to death do go:
　　But not yet for no manner of danger.
EVERYMAN. Gramercy, Knowledge, with all my heart.
KNOWLEDGE. Nay, yet I will not from hence depart,
　　Till I see where ye shall be come.
EVERYMAN. Methinketh, alas, that I must be gone,
　　To make my reckoning and my debts pay,
　　For I see my time is nigh spent away.
　　Take example, all ye that this do hear or see,
　　How they that I loved best do forsake me,
　　Except my Good-Deeds that bideth truly.
GOOD-DEEDS. All earthly things is but vanity:
　　Beauty, Strength, and Discretion, do man forsake,
　　Foolish friends and kinsmen, that fair spake,
　　All fleeth save Good-Deeds, and that am I.
EVERYMAN. Have mercy on me, God most mighty;
　　And stand by me, thou Mother and Maid, holy Mary.
GOOD-DEEDS. Fear not, I will speak for thee.
EVERYMAN. Here I cry God mercy.
GOOD-DEEDS. Short our end, and minish our pain;
　　Let us go and never come again.
EVERYMAN. Into thy hands, Lord, my soul I commend;
　　Receive it, Lord, that it be not lost;
　　As thou me boughtest, so me defend,
　　And save me from the fiend's boast,
　　That I may appear with that blessed host
　　That shall be saved at the day of doom.
　　In manus tuas—of might's most
　　For ever—commendo spiritum meum.
KNOWLEDGE. Now hath he suffered that we all shall endure;
　　The Good-Deeds shall make all sure.
　　Now hath he made ending;
　　Methinketh that I hear angels sing
　　And make great joy and melody,

Where Everyman's soul received shall be.

ANGEL. Come, excellent elect spouse to Jesu:
 Hereabove thou shalt go
 Because of thy singular virtue:
 Now the soul is taken the body fro;
 Thy reckoning is crystal-clear.
 Now shalt thou into the heavenly sphere,
 Unto the which all ye shall come
 That liveth well before the day of doom.

DOCTOR. This moral men may have in mind;
 Ye hearers, take it of worth, old and young,
 And forsake pride, for he deceiveth you in the end,
 And remember Beauty, Five-wits, Strength, and Discretion,
 They all at the last do Everyman forsake,
 Save his Good-Deeds, there doth he take.
 But beware, and they be small
 Before God, he hath no help at all.
 None excuse may be there for Everyman:
 Alas, how shall he do then?
 For after death amends may no man make,
 For then mercy and pity do him forsake.
 If his reckoning be not clear when he do come,
 God will say—ite maledicti in ignem æternum.
 And he that hath his account whole and sound,
 High in heaven he shall be crowned;
 Unto which place God bring us all thither
 That we may live body and soul together.
 Thereto help the Trinity,
 Amen, say ye, for saint Charity.

THUS ENDETH THIS MORAL PLAY OF EVERYMAN.

The Chester Pageant of the Deluge

CHARACTERS

GOD
NOAH
SHEM
HAM
JAPHET
NOAH'S WIFE
SHEM'S WIFE
HAM'S WIFE
JAPHET'S WIFE

THE CHESTER PAGEANT OF THE WATER-LEADERS AND
DRAWERS OF THE DEE CONCERNING NOAH'S DELUGE

GOD. I, God, that all the world have wrought
    Heaven and Earth, and all of nought,
    I see my people, in deed and thought,
    Are foully set in sin.
      My ghost shall not lodge in any man
    That through fleshly liking is my fone,[18]
    But till six score years be gone
    To look if they will blynne.[19]
      Man that I made I will destroy,
    Beast, worm, and fowl to fly,
    For on earth they me annoy,
    The folk that is thereon.
      For it harms me so hurtfully
    The malice now that can multiply,
    That sore it grieveth me inwardly,
    That ever I made man.
      Therefore Noah, my servant free,
    That righteous man art, as I see,
    A ship soon thou shalt make thee,
    Of trees dry and light.
      Little chambers therein thou make
    And binding slich[20] also thou take
    Within and out, thou not slake

---

[18] foe.
[19] cease.
[20] slime, or pitch.

To annoint it through all thy might.
  Three hundred cubits it shall be long,
And so of breadth to make it strong,
Of height so, then must thou fonge,[21]
Thus measure it about.
  One window work though thy might;
One cubit of length and breadth make it,
Upon the side a door shall fit
For to come in and out.
  Eating-places thou make also,
Three roofed chambers, one or two:
For with water I think to stow[22]
Man that I can make.
  Destroyed all the world shall be,
Save thou, thy wife, and sons three,
And all their wives, also, with thee,
Shall saved be for thy sake.

NOAH. Ah, Lord! I thank thee, loud and still,
  That to me art in such will,
And spares me and my house to spill
As now I soothly find.
  Thy bidding, Lord, I shall fulfil,
And never more thee grieve nor grill[23]
That such grace has sent me till
Among all mankind.
  Have done you men and women all;
Help, for aught that may befall,
To work this ship, chamber, and hall,
As God hath bidden us do.

SHEM. Father, I am already bowne,[24]
  An axe I have, by my crown!
As sharp as any in all this town
For to go thereto.

HAM. I have a hatchet, wonder keen,
  To bite well, as may be seen,
A better ground one, as I ween,
Is not in all this town.

JAPHET. And I can well make a pin,
  And with this hammer knock it in;
Go and work without more din;
And I am ready bowne.[24]

---

[21] take.

[22] hinder, stop.

[23] vex.

[24] prepared.

NOAH'S WIFE. And we shall bring timber too,
    For women nothing else to do
    Women be weak to undergo
    Any great travail.
SHEM'S WIFE. Here is a good hackstock;
    On this you must hew and knock:
    Shall none be idle in this flock,
    Nor now may no man fail.
HAM'S WIFE. And I will go to gather slich,[25]
    The ship for to clean and pitch;
    Anointed it must be, every stitch,
    Board, tree, and pin.
JAPHET'S WIFE. And I will gather chips here
    To make a fire for you, in fear,
    And for to dight[26] your dinner,
    Against you come in.

    [*Here they make signs as though they were working divers instruments.*]

NOAH. Now in the name of God I will begin,
    To make the ship that we shall in,
    That we be ready for to swim,
    At the coming of the flood.
      These boards I join together,
    To keep us safe from the weather
    That we may roam both hither and thither
    And safe be from this flood.
      Of this tree will I have the mast,
    Tied with gables that will last
    With a sail yard for each blast
    And each thing in its kind.
      With topmast high and bowsprit.
    With cords and ropes, I hold all fit
    To sail forth at the next weete[27]
    This ship is at an end.
    Wife in this castle we shall be kept:
    My children and thou I would in leaped!
NOAH'S WIFE. In faith, Noe, I had as lief thou had slept, for all thy
      frankishfare,[28]

---

[25] slime, mud.
[26] prepare.
[27] tide.
[28] nonsense.

For I will not do after thy rede.[29]

NOAH. Good wife, do as I thee bid.

NOAH'S WIFE. By Christ not, or I see more need,
    Though thou stand all the day and rave.

NOAH. Lord, that women be crabbed aye!
    And never are meek, that I dare say.
    This is well seen of me to-day
    In witness of you each one.
      Good wife, let be all this beere[30]
    That thou makest in this place here,
    For they all ween thou art master;
    And so thou art, by St. John!

GOD. Noah, take thou thy company
    And in the ship hie that you be,
    For none so righteous man to me
    Is now on earth living.
      Of clean beasts with thee thou take
    Seven and seven, or thou seake,
    He and she make to make
    Quickly in that thou bring.
      Of beasts unclean two and two,
    Male and female, without more;
    Of clean fowls seven also,
    The he and she together.
      Of fowles unclean two, and no more;
    Of beasts as I said before:
    That shall be saved through my lore
    Against I send the weather.
      Of all meats that must be eaten
    Into the ship look there be gotten,
    For that no way may be forgotten
    And do all this by deene.[31]
      To sustain man and beasts therein,
    Aye, till the waters cease and blyn.[32]
    This world is filled full of sin
    And that is now well seen.
      Seven days be yet coming,
    You shall have space them in to bring;
    After that it is my liking
    Mankind for to annoy.
      Forty days and forty nights,

---

[29] advice.

[30] noise.

[31] immediately.

[32] stop.

Rain shall fall for their unrights;
And that I have made through my might,
Now think I to destroy.

NOAH. Lord, at your bidding I am bayne,[33]
Since none other grace will gain,
It will I fulfil fain,
For gracious I thee find.

A hundred winters and twenty
This ship making tarried have I:
If, through amendment, any mercy
Would fall unto mankind.

Have done, you men and women all.
Hie you, lest this water fall,
That each beast were in his stall
And into ship brought.

Of clean beasts seven shall be;
Of unclean two, this God bade me;
This flood is nigh, well may we see,
Therefore tarry you nought.

SHEM. Sir, here are lions, leopards in,
Horses, mares, oxen, and swine,
Goats, calves, sheep, and kine,
Here sitten[34] may you see.

HAM. Camels, asses, men may find;
Buck, doe, hart and hind,
And beasts of all manner kind.
Here be, as thinks me.

JAPHET. Take here cats and dogs too,
Otter, fox, fulmart also;
Hares, hopping gaily, can ye
Have kail here for to eat.

NOAH'S WIFE. And here are bears, wolves set,
Apes, owls, marmoset;
Weasels, squirrels, and ferret
Here they eat their meat.

SHEM'S WIFE. Yet more beasts are in this house!
Here cats come in full crowse,[35]
Here a rat and here a mouse;
They stand nigh together.

HAM'S WIFE. And here are fowls less and more,
Herons, cranes and bittern;

---

[33] ready.
[34] settled.
[35] comfortable.

Swans, peacocks, have them before!
Meat for this weather.
JAPHET'S WIFE. Here are cocks, kites, crows,
Rooks, ravens, many rows;
Cuckoos, curlews, whoso knows,
Each one in his kind.
And here are doves, ducks, drakes,
Redshanks, running through the lakes,
And each fowl that language makes
In this ship men may find.

[*In the stage direction the sons of* NOAH *are enjoined to mention
aloud the names of the animals which enter; a representation
of which, painted on parchment, is to be carried by the
actors.*]

NOAH. Wife, come in, why standest thou there?
Thou art ever forward, that I dare swear:
Come on God's half, time it were,
For fear lest that we drown.
NOAH'S WIFE. Yea, sir, set up your sail
And row forth with evil heale,
For, without any fail,
I will not out of this town.
But I have my gossips every one,
One foot further I will not go;
They shall not drown, by St. John!
If I may save their life.
They loved me full well, by Christ!
But thou wilt let them in thy chest,
Else row forth, Noah, whither thou list,
And get thee a new wife.
NOAH. Shem, some love thy mother, 'tis true;
Forsooth, such another I do not know!
SHEM. Father, I shall set her in, I trow,
Without any fail.
Mother, my father after thee sends,
And bids thee unto yonder ship wend,[36]
Look up and see the wind,
For we be ready to sail.
NOAH'S WIFE. Son, go again to him and say
I will not come therein to-day!
NOAH. Come in, wife, in twenty devils' way,

---

[36] go.

Or else stand without.

HAM. Shall we all fetch her in?

NOAH. Yea, sons, in Christ's blessing and mine,
    I would you hied you betime,
    For of this flood I am in doubt.

JAPHET. Mother, we pray you altogether,
    For we are here, your children;
    Come into the ship for fear of the weather,
    For his love that you bought!

NOAH'S WIFE. That I will not for your call,
    But if I have my gossips all.

GOSSIP. The flood comes in full fleeting fast,
    On every side it broadens in haste;
    For fear of drowning I am aghast:
    Good gossip, let me come in!
       Or let us drink ere we depart,
    For oftentimes we have done so;
    For at a time thou drinkst a quart,
    And so will I ere that I go.

SHEM. In faith, mother, yet you shall,
    Whether you will or not!

    [*She goes.*]

NOAH. Welcome, wife, into this boat!

NOAH'S WIFE. And have them that for thy note![37]

    [*Et dat alapam victa.*[38]]

NOAH. Aha! marry, this is hot!
    It is good to be still.
    My children! methinks this boat removes!
    Our tarrying here hugely me grieves!
    Over the land the water spreads!
    God do as he will!
       Ah, great God, thou art so good!
    Now all this world is in a flood
    As I see well in sight.
       This window will I close anon,
    And into my chamber will I gone
    Till this water, so great one,
    Be slakèd through thy might.

---

[37] Business, occupation.

[38] And being conquered she deals a slap.

[NOAH, *according to stage directions, is now to shut the windows
of the ark and retire for a short time. He is then to chant the
psalm, Salva me, Domine! and afterwards to open them and
look out.*]

Now forty days are fully gone.
Send a raven I will anon;
If aught were earth, tree, or stone,
Be dry in any place.
    And if this fowl come not again
It is a sign, sooth to say,
That dry it is on hill or plain,
And God hath done some grace.

[*A raven is now despatched.*]

    Ah, Lord! wherever this raven lie,
Somewhere is dry well I see;
But yet a dove, by my lewtye[39]
After I will send.
Thou wilt turn again to me
For of all fowls that may fly
Thou art most meek and hend.[40]

[*The stage direction enjoins here that another dove shall be ready
with an olive branch in its mouth, which is to be dropped by
means of a cord into NOAH'S hand.*]

Ah Lord! blessed be thou aye,
That me hast comforted thus to-day!
By this sight, I may well say
This flood begins to cease.
    My sweet dove to me brought has
A branch of olive from some place;
This betokeneth God has done us some grace,
And is a sign of peace.
    Ah, Lord! honoured must thou be!
All earth dries now I see;
But yet, till thou command me,
Hence will I not hie.
    All this water is away,

---

[39] fidelity.
[40] kind.

Therefore as soon as I may
Sacrifice I shall do in faye[41]
To thee devoutly.
GOD. Noah, take thy wife anon,
And thy children every one,
Out of the ship thou shalt gone,
And they all with thee.
Beasts and all that can flie,
Out anon they shall hie,
On earth to grow and multiply:
I will that it be so.
NOAH. Lord, I thank thee, through thy might,
Thy bidding shall be done in hight,[42]
And, as fast as I may dight[43]
I will do thee honour.
  And to thee offer sacrifice,
Therefore comes in all wise,
For of these beasts that be his
Offer I will this stower.[44]

[*Then leaving the ark with his whole family, he shall take the
animals and birds, make an offering of them, and set out on
his way.*]

  Lord God, in majesty,
That such grace has granted me,
When all was borne safe to be,
Therefore now I am boune.[45]
  My wife, my children, my company,
With sacrifice to honour thee,
With beasts, fowls, as thou may see,
I offer here right soon.
GOD. Noah, to me thou art full able,
And thy sacrifice acceptable,
For I have found thee true and stable,
On thee now must I myn.[46]
Curse earth will I no more
That man's sin it grieves sore,
For of youth man full of yore

---

[41] faith.
[42] haste.
[43] prepare.
[44] steer. .
[45] ready.
[46] Thee now must I have in mind.

Has been inclined to sin.
 You shall now grow and multiply
And earth you edify,
Each beast and fowl that may flie
Shall be afraid for you.
 And fish in sea that may flitt
Shall sustain you—I you behite[47]
To eat of them you not lett[48]
That clean be you may know.
 There as you have eaten before
Grasses and roots, since you were born,
Of clean beasts, less and more,
I give you leave to eat.
 Save blood and fish both in fear
Of wrong dead carrion that is here,
Eat not of that in no manner,
For that aye you shall lett.[49]
 Manslaughter also you shall flee,
For that is not pleasant to me
That sheds blood, he or she
Ought where among mankind.
 That sheds blood, his blood shall be
And vengeance have, that men shall see;
Therefore now beware now all ye
You fall not in that sin.
And forward now with you I make
And all thy seed, for thy sake,
Of such vengeance for to slake,
For now I have my will.
 Here I promise thee a behest,[50]
That man, woman, fowl, nor beast
With water while the world shall last,
I will no more spill.
 My bow between you and me
In the firmament shall be,
By very tokens, that you may see
That such vengeance shall cease.
 That man, nor woman, shall never more
Be wasted by water, as is before,
But for sin that grieveth sore,
Therefore this vengeance was.

---

[47] promise.
[48] cease.
[49] leave.
[50] covenant.

Where clouds in the welkin
That each bow shall be seen,
In token that my wrath or tene[51]
Should never this wroken be.

The string is turned toward you,
And toward me bent is the bow,
That such weather shall never show,
And this do I grant to thee.

My blessing now I give thee here,
To thee Noah, my servant dear;
For vengeance shall no more appear;
And now farewell, my darling dear!

---

[51] anger.

The Chester Pageant Of Abraham, Melchisedec, And Isaac

CHARACTERS

GOD
ABRAHAM
LOT
ISAAC
MELCHISEDEC
A KNIGHT
EXPOSITOR
A MESSENGER

THE CHESTER PAGEANT OF THE BARBERS AND WAX-CHANDLERS REPRESENTING ABRAHAM, MELCHISEDEC, AND ISAAC

Abraham, newly returned from the slaughter of the four kings, meets Melchisedec riding.

PRELUDE

MESSENGER. All peace, Lordings, that be present,
    And hearken now with good intent,
    How Noah away from us he went
      With all his company;
    And Abraham, through God's grace,
    He is come forth into this place,
    And you will give him room and space
      To tell you his storye.
    This play, forsooth, begin shall he,
    In worship of the Trinity,
    That you may all hear and see
      What shall be done to-day.
    My name is Gobbet-on-the-Green,
    No longer here I may be seen,
    Farewell, my Lordings, all by dene[52]
      For letting[53] of your play. [*Exit.*]

[*Enter* ABRAHAM.]

---

[52] in haste.
[53] hindering.

ABRAHAM. Ah! thou high God, granter of grace
    That ending nor beginning has,
    I thank thee, Lord, that to me has
      To-day given victory.
    Lot, my brother, that taken was,
    I have restored him in this case,
    And brought him home into his place
      Through thy might and mastery.
    To worship thee I will not wond,[54]
    That four kings of uncouth land
    To-day hast sent into my hand,
      And of riches great array.
    Therefore of all that I can win
    To give thee tithe I will begin,
    When I the city soon come in,
      And share with thee my prey.
    Melchisedec, that here king is
    And God's priest also, I wis,
    The tithe I will give him of this,
      As just is, what I do.
    God who has sent me victory
    O'er four kings graciously,
    With him my spoil share will I,
      The city, when I come to.
LOT. Abraham, brother, I thank it thee,
    Who this day hast delivered me
    From enemies' hands, and their postye,[55]
      And saved me from woe!
    Therefore I will give tithing
    Of my goods while I am living,
    And now also of his sending,
      Tithe I will give also.

[*Then comes a knight to* MELCHISEDEC.]

Knight. My lord, the king's tidings aright
    Your heart for to gladden and light:
    Abraham hath slain in fight
      Four kings, since he went.
    Here he will be this same night,
    And riches with him enough dight.

---

[54] fail.
[55] might.

I heard him thank God Almight
For grace he had him sent.

MELCHISEDEC. [*stretching his hand to heaven.*] Ah! blessed be God
    that is but one!
Against Abraham I will be gone
Worshipfully, and then anon,
    My office to fulfil,
Will present him with bread and wine,
For, grace of God is him within;
Speeds fast for love mine!
    For this is God's will.

KNIGHT. [*with a cup.*] Sir, here is wine withouten were,[56]
And thereto bread, both white and clear,
To present him in good manere
    That so us helped has.

MELCHISEDEC. To God, I know he is full dear,
For of all things his prayer
He hath, without danger,
And specially great grace.

[MELCHISEDEC *coming to* ABRAHAM *and offering him a cup of
wine and bread on a plate.*]

Abraham, welcome must thou be,
God's grace is fully in thee,
Blessed ever must thou be
    That enemies so can make.
I have brought, as thou may'st see,
Bread and wine for thy degree;
Receive this present now from me,
    And that I thee beseke.[57]

ABRAHAM. Sir king, welcome in good say,
Thy present is welcome to my pay.
God has helpéd me to-day
    Unworthy though I were.
He shall have part of my prey
That I won since I went away.
Therefore to thee thou take it may
    The tenth I offer here.

[*He delivers to the King a laden horse.*]

---

[56] without suspicion.
[57] beseech.

MELCHISEDEC. And your present, sir, take I,
    And honour it devoutly,
    For much good it may signify
        In time that is coming.
    Therefore horse, harness, and peryé,[58]
    As falls to my dignity,
    The tithe of it I take of thee,
        And receive thy off'ring.

[ABRAHAM *receives the bread and wine, and* MELCHISEDEC *the*
    laden horse as tithe from LOT.]

LOT. And I will offer with good intent
    Of such goods as God hath me sent
    To Melchisedec here present,
        As God's will is to be.
    Abraham, my brother, offered has;
    And so will I with God's grace:
    This royal cup before your face,
        Receive it now of me.

[LOT *offers the wine and bread, which* MELCHISEDEC *receives.*]

MELCHISEDEC. Sir, your off'ring welcome is,
    And well I know forsooth, I wis,
    That fully God's will it is
        That is now done to-day.
    Go we together to my city,
    And now God heartily thank we
    That helps us aye through his postye,[59]
        For so we full well may.
EXPOSITOR. [*riding.*] Lordings, what may this signify,
    I will expound openly
    That all, standing hereby,
        May know what this may be.
    This off'ring, I say verament,[60]
    Signifieth the new Testament,
    That now is used with good intent
        Throughout all Christianity.
    In the old law without leasing,[61]
    When these two good men were living,

---

[58] precious stones.
[59] might.
[60] verily.
[61] leasing.

Of beasts was all their off'ring
 And eke their sacrament.
But since Christ died on the rood-tree,
With bread and wine him worship we,
And on Shrove Thursday in his Maundy[62]
 Was his commandment.
But for this thing used should be
Afterward as now done we,
In signification, believe you me,
 Melchisedec did so;
And tithes-making, as you see here,
Of Abraham beginning were.
Therefore he was to God full dear,
 And so were they both too.
By Abraham understand I may
The father of heaven in good fay,[63]
Melchisedec a priest to his pay
 To minister that sacrament
That Christ ordained on Shrove Thursday
In bread and wine to honour him aye;
This signifieth, the truth to say,
 Melchisedec's present.

GOD. Abraham, my servant, I say to thee,
 Thy help and succour I will be,
 For thy good deed much pleaseth me,
 I tell thee surely.

ABRAHAM. Lord, one thing that thou wilt see,
 That I pray after with heart free,
 Grant me, Lord, through thy postye:[64]
  Some fruit of my body!
 I have no child, foul nor fair,
 Save my Nurry[65] to be my heir,
 That makes me greatly to apayre.[66]
  On me, Lord, have mercy!

GOD. My friend, Abraham, leave thou me.
 Thy Nurry thine heir shall not be,
 But one son I shall send thee,
  Begotten of thy body.
 Abraham, do as I thee say:
 Look up and tell,[67] and if thou may,

---

[62] bequest: "Maundy" really meant "command."
[63] faith.
[64] might.
[65] nurseling, foster-child.
[66] lament.

Stars standing on the stray;
 That impossible were.
No more shalt thou, for no need,
Number of thy body the seed
That thou shalt have withouten dreed,
 Thou art to me so dear.
Wherefore, Abraham, servant free,
Look that thou be true to me,
And fore-word here I make with thee
 Thy seed to multiply.
So much more further shalt thou be,
Kings of thy seed men shall see,
And one child of great degree
 All mankind shall forby.[68]
I will that from henceforth alway
Each knave's child on the eighth day
Be circumcised, as I say,
 And thou thyself full soon;
And who circumcised not is
Forsaken shall be by me, I wis;
For disobedient that man is,
 Therefore look that this be done.
ABRAHAM. Lord, already in good fay[69]
 Blessed be thou, ever and aye;
For that men truly know may
 Thy folk from other men,
Circumcised they shall be all
Anon for aught that may befall.
I thank thee, Lord, thy own thrall,
 Kneeling on my knee'n.
EXPOSITOR. Lordings all take good intent
 What betokens this commandment:
This was some time a sacrament
 In th' old law truly ta'en.
As followeth now verament,[70]
So was this in the old Testament;
But when Christ, away it went,
 And baptism then began.
Also God promises here
To Abraham, his servant dear,
So much seed that in no manere

---

[67] count.
[68] fore-buy (pre-purchase with his blood).
[69] faith.
[70] verily.

Number'd it might be.
And one seed, mankind to forby,
That was Jesus Christ witterlye[71]
For of his kind was our Lady,
And so also was he.
GOD. Abraham, my servant Abraham.
ABRAHAM. Lo, Lord, already here I am.
GOD. Take Isaac, thy son by name
That thou lovest best of all
And in sacrifice offer him to me
Upon that hill, beside thee.
Abraham, I will that it so be
For aught that may befall.
ABRAHAM. My lord, to thee is my intent
Ever to be obedient,
That son that thou to me hast sent,
Offer I will to thee.
And fulfil thy commandment
With hearty will, as I am kent
High God, Lord Omnipotent,
Thy bidding done shall be.
My menye[72] and my children each one
Lingers at home, both all and one,
Save Isaac shall with me gone
To a hill here beside.

[*Enter* ISAAC.]

ABRAHAM. Make thee ready, my darling,
For we must do a little thing.
This wood upon thy back thou bring,
We must not long abide.
A sword and fire I will take,
For sacrifice I must make;
God's bidding will I not forsake,
But aye obedient be.
ISAAC. Father, I am all ready
To do your bidding meekly,
To bear this wood full bound am I,
As you command me.
ABRAHAM. O Isaac, Isaac, my darling dear,
My blessing now I give thee here.

---

[71] truly.
[72] household.

Take up this faggot with good cheer,
  And on thy back it bring,
  And fire with me I will take.
ISAAC. Your bidding I will not forsake,
  Father, I will never slake[73]
    To fulfil your bidding.

[ISAAC *takes the wood on his back, and they set out for the hill.*]

ABRAHAM. Now Isaac, son, go we our way
  To yonder mountain, if that we may.
ISAAC. My dear father, I will essay
  To follow you full fain.
ABRAHAM. Oh! my heart will break in three,
  To hear thy words I have pity.
  As thou wilt, Lord, so must it be:
    To thee I will be bane.
  Lay down thy faggot my own son dear!
ISAAC. All ready, father, lo, it is here.
  But why make you so heavy cheer?
    Are you anything adread?
  Father, if it be your will,
  Where is the beast that we shall kill?
ABRAHAM. There is none, son, upon this hill
  That I see here in this stead.
ISAAC. Father, I am full sore afraid
  To see you bare this naked sword.
  I hope for all middle-yard[74]
  You will not slay your child.
ABRAHAM. Dread thee not, my child, I read
  Our Lord will send of his godhead
  Some kind of beast in thy stead,
    Either tame or wild.
ISAAC. Father, tell me, or I go,
  Whether I shall have harm or no.
ABRAHAM. Ah, dear God, that me is woe!
  Thou bursts my heart in sunder.
ISAAC. Father, tell me of this case,
  Why you your drawn sword has,
  And bare it naked in this place;
    Thereof I have great wonder.
ABRAHAM. Isaac, son, peace! I pray thee,

---

[73] be slack, or slow.
[74] "middle-yard,"—farm-yard: i.e. instead of all creatures from the farm-yard.

Thou breaks my heart even in three.

ISAAC. I pray you, father, leave nothing from me,
    But tell me what you think.

ABRAHAM. O Isaac, Isaac, I must thee kill.

ISAAC. Alas! father, is that your will,
    Your own child here for to spill,
      Upon this hill's brink?
    If I have trespassed in any degree,
    With a rod you may beat me;
    Put up your sword, if your will be,
      For I am but a child.

ABRAHAM. Oh, my son! I am sorry
    To do to thee this great annoy,
    God's commandment do must I,
      His works are aye full mild.

ISAAC. Would God, my mother were here with me!
    She would kneel upon her knee,
    Praying you, father, if it might be,
    For to save my life.

ABRAHAM. Oh, comely creature, but I thee kill,
    I grieve my God, and that full ill:
    I may not work against his will
      But ever obedient be.
    O Isaac, son, to thee I say:
    God has commanded me this day
    Sacrifice—this is no nay—
      To make of thy body.

ISAAC. Is it God's will I should be slain?

ABRAHAM. Yea, son, it is not for to layne;[75]
    To his bidding I will be bane,[76]
      Ever to his pleasing.
    But that I do this doleful deed,
    My Lord will not quit[77] me my meed.[78]

ISAAC. Marry! father, God forbid
    But you do your off'ring.
    Father, at home your sons you shall find
    That you must love by course of kind.
    Be I once out of your mind,
      Your sorrow may soon cease,
    But you must do God's bidding.
    Father, tell my mother of nothing.

---

[75] hesitate.
[76] obedient.
[77] deny.
[78] reward.

ABRAHAM. For sorrow I may my hands wring,
    Thy mother I cannot please.
  O Isaac, blessed may'st thou be!
  Almost my wit I lose for thee,
  The blood of thy body so free
    I feel full loth to shed.
ISAAC. Father, since you must needs do so,
  Let it pass lightly and overgo;
  Kneeling on my knees two,
    Your blessing on me spread!
ABRAHAM. My blessing, dear son, give I thee
  And thy mother's with heart so free;
  The blessing of the Trinity,
    My dear son, on thee light!
ISAAC. Father, I pray you hide mine een
  That I see not your sword so keen;
  Your stroke, father, I would not seen,
    Lest I against it thrill.
ABRAHAM. My dear son Isaac, speak no more,
  Thy words make my heart full sore.
ISAAC. O dear father, wherefore, wherefore?
    Since I must needs be dead,
  One thing I would you pray:
  Since I must die the death this day,
  As few strokes as you may,
    When you smite off my head.
ABRAHAM. Thy meekness, child, makes me afray;[79]
  My song may be "Well away!"
ISAAC. O, dear father, do away
    Your making so mickle moan!
  Now truly, father, this talking
  Doth but make long tarrying.
  I pray you come and make ending
    And let me hence gone!
ABRAHAM. Come hither, my child, that art so sweet:
  Thou must be bound now, hand and feet.

    [*Binding* ISAAC.]

ISAAC. Ah, father! we must no more meet
  By aught that I can see,
  But do with me just as you will,
  I must obey, and that is skill,

---

[79] afraid.

God's commandment to fulfil,
   For needs so must it be.
Upon the purpose that have set you,
Forsooth, father, I will not let you,
But evermore unto you bow,
   While that I may.
Father, greet well my brethren young,
And pray my mother for her blessing,
I come no more under her wing:
   Farewell for ever and aye!
But, father, I cry you mercy,
Of that I have trespassed·to thee,
Forgiven, father, that it may be
   Until doom's day.

ABRAHAM. My dear son, let be thy moans;
   My child, thou grievedst me but once.
   Blessed be thou body and bones,
     And I forgive thee here.
   Lo, my dear son, here shalt thou lie;
   Unto my work now must I hie,
   I had as lief myself to die
     As thou, my darling dear.

ISAAC. Father, if you be to me kind,
   About my head a kercher[80] bind,
   And let me lightly out of your mind,
     And soon that I were sped.

ABRAHAM. Farewell, my sweet son of grace!

ISAAC. I pray you, father, turn down my face
   A little while, while you have space,
     For I am full sore adread.

ABRAHAM. To do this deed I am sorry.

ISAAC. Yea, Lord, to thee I call and cry:
   On my soul may thou have mercy,
     Heartily I thee pray.

ABRAHAM. Lord, I would fain work thy will.
   This young innocent that lies so still
   Full loth were I him to kill
     By any manner of way.

ISAAC. My dear father, I you pray,
   Let me take my clothes away,
   For shedding blood on them to-day,
     At my last ending.

ABRAHAM. Heart! if thou would'st break in three,

---

[80] kerchief.

Thou shalt never master me,
I will no longer let[81] for thee,
   My God I may not grieve.
ISAAC. Ah, mercy, father! why tarry you so?
Smite off my head, and let me go!
I pray you, rid me of my woe;
   For now I take my leave.
ABRAHAM. Ah, son! my heart will break in three
To hear thee speak such words to me.
Jesus, on me thou have pitý
   That I have most in mind!
ISAAC. Now, father, I see that I shall die,
Almighty God in majestý,
My soul I offer unto thee:
   Lord, to it be kind.

[ABRAHAM *takes the sword, as if to kill his son, when two angels*
   appear. One of them seizes the point of the sword, and says:]

1ST ANGEL. Abraham, my servant dear!
ABRAHAM. Lo, Lord! I am already here.
1ST ANGEL. Lay not thy sword in any manner
   On Isaac, thy dear darling!
Nay! do thou him no annoy!
For thou dreadest God; well, see I,
That of thy son hast no mercy
   To fulfil his bidding.
2ND ANGEL. And for his bidding thou doest aye,
And spares neither, for fear nor fray,
To do thy son to death to-day,
   Isaac to thee full dear,
Therefore God has sent by me in fay,[82]
A lamb that is both good and gay
Into this place as thou see may,
   Lo! it is right here.
ABRAHAM. Ah, Lord of heaven and king of bliss!
Thy bidding I shall do, I wis.
Sacrifice here to me sent is
   And all, Lord, through thy grace.
A horned wether here I see,
Among the briars tied is he,
To thee offered it shall be

---

[81] hesitate, delay.
[82] in good faith.

Anon, right in this place.

[*Let* ABRAHAM *sacrifice the ram.*]

GOD. Abraham, by myself I swear,
For thou hast been obedient ever,
And spared not thy son so dear,
   To fulfil my bidding,
Thou shalt be blessed, thou art worthy,
Thy seed I shall multiply,
As stars and sand so many het I,[83]
   Of thy body coming.
Of enemies thou shalt have power,
And thy blood also in fear,
For thou has been meek and boneer[84]
   To do as I thee bade.
And all nations leave thou me,
Blessed evermore shall be
Through fruit that shall come of thee
   And saved through thy seed.

THE EPILOGUE

EXPOSITOR. Lordings, the signification
   Of this deed of devotion,
   An you will, it is shewn,
     May turn you to much good.
This deed you see done in this place,
In example of Jesus done it was,
That for to win mankind grace
     Was sacrificed on the rood.
By Abraham you may understand
The Father of heaven that can fand[85]
With his son's blood to break that band
     The devil had brought us to.
By Isaac understand I may
Jesus who was obedient aye,
His father's will to work alway,
     His death to undergo.

---

[83] promised I.
[84] debonair.
[85] find, find means.

The Wakefield Second Shepherds' Play

CHARACTERS

1ST SHEPHERD
2ND SHEPHERD
3RD SHEPHERD
MAC, THE SHEEP-STEALER
MAC'S WIFE, GILL
MARY
THE CHILD CHRIST
AN ANGEL

THE WAKEFIELD SECOND NATIVITY PLAY

1ST SHEPHERD. Lord! what, these weathers are cold, and I am ill
   happed;
I am near hand-dold,[86] so long have I napped;
My legs bend and fold, my fingers are chapped,
It is not as I would, for I am all lapped
   In sorrow.
In storms and tempest,
Now in the east, now in the west,
Woe is him has never rest,
   Mid day nor morrow.
But we silly shepherds, that walk upon the moor,
In faith, we are near hands out of the door;
No wonder, as it stands, if we be poor,
For the tilth of our lands lies fallow as the floor,
We are so lamed,
So taxed and shamed,
We are made hand-tamed,
   With these gentlery-men.
Thus they rieve us of rest, Our Lady them wary,
These men that are lord-fest,[87] they cause the plough tarry.
That men say is for the best, we find it contrary,
Thus are husbands[88] opprest, in point to miscarry,
   In life.
Thus hold they us under,
Thus they bring us in blunder,

---

[86] numb of hand.
[87] fast tied (to a lord, as a public-house to a brewer).
[88] husbandmen.

It were great wonder,
     And ever should we thrive.
For may he get a paint sleeve,[89] or a brooch now on days,
Woe is he that shall grieve, or once again says,
Dare no man him reprieve, what mast'ry he has,
And yet may none believe one word that he says—
     No letter.
He can make purveyance,
With boast and bragance,[90]
And all through maintenance,
     Of men that are greater.
There shall come a swain, as proud as a po,[91]
He must borrow my wain, my plough also,
Then I am full fain to grant or he go.
Thus live we in pain, anger, and woe,
     By night and day;
He must have if he longéd
If I should forgang[92] it,
I were better be hangéd
     Than once say him nay.
It does me good, as I walk thus by mine own,
Of this world for to talk in manner of moan
To my sheep will I stalk and hearken anon
There abide on a balk, or sit on a stone
     Full soon.
For I trow, pardie!
True men if they be,
We get more company
     Or it be noon.
2ND SHEPHERD. "Beniste"[93] and "Dominus!" what may this bemean?
Why fares this world thus, oft have we not seen.
Lord, these weathers are spitous,[94] and the weather full keen;
And the frost so hideous they water mine een,
     No lie.
Now in dry, now in wet,
Now in snow, now in sleet,
When my shoon freeze to my feet
     It is not all easy.
But as far as I ken, or yet as I go,

---

[89] a painted sleeve.
[90] bragging.
[91] peacock.
[92] forego.
[93] Benedicite.
[94] spiteful.

We silly wed-men dree mickle woe;[95]
We have sorrow then and then, it falls often so,
Silly capyl, our hen, both to and fro
    She cackles,
But begin she to croak,
To groan or to cluck,
Woe is him, say of our cock,
    For he is in the shackles.
These men that are wed, have not all their will,
When they are full hard sted,[96] they sigh full still;
God wait they are led full hard and full ill,
In bower nor in bed they say not there till
    This tide.
My part have I found,
My lesson is learn'd,
Woe is him that is bound,
    For he must abide.
But now late in our lives, a marvel to me,
That I think my heart rives,[97] such wonders to see,
What that destiny drives it should so be,
Some men will have two wives, and some men three,
    In store.
Some are woe that have any;
But so far ken I,
Woe is he who has many,
    For he feels it sore.
But young men of wooing, for God that you bought,
Be well ware of wedding, and think in your thought
"Had I wist" is a thing it serves ye of nought;
Mickle still mourning has wedding home brought,
    And griefs,
With many a sharp shower,
For thou may catch in an hour
That shall serve thee full sour
    As long as thou lives.
For as read I epistle, I have one to my fear
As sharp as a thistle, as rough as a brere.[98]
She is browed like a bristle with a sour lenten cheer;
Had she once wet her whistle she could sing full clear
    Her pater-noster.
She is as great as a whale,

---

[95] we silly wedded men endure much woe.
[96] placed, bestead.
[97] is riven asunder.
[98] briar.

She has a gallon of gall;
By him that died for us all!
  I would I had run till I lost her.
1ST SHEPHERD. God look over the row, full deafly ye stand.
2ND SHEPHERD. Yea, the devil in thy maw!—so tariand,[99]
  Saw thou aught now of Daw?
1ST SHEPHERD. Yea, on a lea land
  Heard I him blow, he comes here at hand,
    Not far;
  Stand still.
2ND SHEPHERD. Why?
1ST SHEPHERD. For he comes here, hope I.
2ND SHEPHERD. He will make us both a lie,
    But if we beware.
3RD SHEPHERD. Christ's cross me speed, and Saint Nicholas!
  Thereof had I need, it is worse than it was.
  Whoso could take heed, and let the world pass,
  It is ever in dread and brittle as glass,
    And slithers,[100]
  This world fared never so,
  With marvels mo and mo,[101]
  Now in weal, now in woe,
    And all things withers.
  Was never since Noah's flood such floods seen,
  Winds and rains so rude, and storms so keen,
  Some stammered, some stood in doubt, as I ween,
  Now God turn all to good, I say as I mean,
    For ponder.
  These floods so they drown
  Both in fields and in town,
  They bear all down,
    And that is a wonder.
  We that walk in the nights, our cattle to keep,
  We see sudden sights, when other men sleep:
  Yet methinks my heart lights, I see shrews peep,
  Ye are two, all wights,[102] I will give my sheep
    A turn.
  But full ill have I meant,
  As I walk on this bent,[103]
  I may lightly repent,

---

[99] tarrying.
[100] slithers, slides away.
[101] more and more.
[102] You are two who wit, or know, all.
[103] field.

My toes if I spurn.
Ah, sir, God you save, and master mine!
A drink fain would I have and somewhat to dine.

1ST SHEPHERD. Christ's curs, my knave, thou art a lazy hyne.[104]

2ND SHEPHERD. What, the boy list rave. Abide until syne[105]
    We have made it.
    I'll thrift on thy pate!
    Though the shrew came late
    Yet is he in state
      To dine if he had it.

3RD SHEPHERD. Such servants as I, that sweats and swinks,
    Eats our bread full dry, and that me forthinks;
    We are oft wet and weary when master men winks,
    Yet comes full lately both dinners and drinks,
      But neatly.
    Both our dame and our sire,
    When we have run in the mire,
    They can nip at our hire,[106]
      And pay us full lately.
    But hear my truth, master, for the fare that ye make
    I shall do thereafter work, as I take;
    I shall do a little, sir, and strive and still lack,
    For yet lay my supper never on my stomack
      In fields.
    Whereto should I threap?[107]
    With my staff can I leap,
    And men say "light cheap
      Letherly for yields."[108]

1ST SHEPHERD. Thou wert an ill lad, to ride on wooing
    With a man that had but little of spending.

2ND SHEPHERD. Peace, boy!—I bade: no more jangling,
    Or I shall make thee afraid, by the heaven's king!
      With thy gawds;
    Where are our sheep, boy, we scorn?

3RD SHEPHERD. Sir, this same day at morn,
    I them left in the corn,
      When they rang lauds;
    They have pasture good, they cannot go wrong.

1ST SHEPHERD. That is right by the rood, these nights are long,
    Yet I would, or we yode,[109] one gave us a song.

---

[104] hind.
[105] till such time as we have made it.
[106] stint our wages.
[107] argue.
[108] a light bargain yields badly.

2ND SHEPHERD. So I thought as I stood, to mirth us among.[110]
3RD SHEPHERD. I grant.
1ST SHEPHERD. Let me sing the tenory.
2ND SHEPHERD. And I the treble so high.
3RD SHEPHERD. Then the mean falls to me;
Let see how ye chaunt.

[MAC *enters, with a cloak thrown over his smock.*]

MAC. Now, Lord, for thy names seven, that made both moon and starns[111]
Well more than I can even: thy will, Lord, of my thorns;
I am all uneven, that moves oft my horns,[112]
Now would God I were in heaven, for there weep no bairns
So still.
1ST SHEPHERD. Who is that pipes so poor?
MAC. Would God ye knew how I fare!
Lo, a man that walks on the moor,
And has not all his will.
2ND SHEPHERD. Mac, where hast thou gone? Tell us tidings.
3RD SHEPHERD. Is he come? Then each one take heed to his things.

[*Takes his cloak from him.*]

MAC. What, I am a yeoman, I tell you, of the king;
The self and the same, sent from a great lording,
And sich.[113]
Fy on you, get thee hence,
Out of my presence,
I must have reverence,
Why, who be ich?[114]
1ST SHEPHERD. Why make ye it so quaint? Mac, ye do wrong.
2ND SHEPHERD. But, Mac, list, ye saint? I trow that ye sang.
3RD SHEPHERD. I trow the shrew can paint, the devil might him hang!
MAC. I shall make complaint, and make you all to thwang.[115]
At a word,
And tell even how ye doth.
1ST SHEPHERD. But, Mac, is that sooth?

---

[109] went.
[110] to make mirth among us.
[111] stars.
[112] "harnes" in original, which may mean "harness."
[113] such (of such).
[114] I.
[115] be thwacked, or flogged.

Now take out that southern tooth,
    And set in a tord.
2ND SHEPHERD. Mac, the devil in your ee,[116] a stroke would I lend you.
3RD SHEPHERD. Mac, know ye not me? By God, I could tell you.
MAC. God look you all three, methought I had seen you.
    Ye are a fair company.
1ST SHEPHERD. Can ye now moan you?
2ND SHEPHERD. Shrew, jape![117]
    Thus late as thou goes,
    What will men suppose?
    And thou hast an ill noise[118]
        Of stealing of sheep.
MAC. And I am true as steel all men wait,
    But a sickness I feel, that holds me full haytt,[119]
    My belly fares not well, it is out of its state.
3RD SHEPHERD. Seldom lies the devil dead by the gate.
MAC. Therefore
    Full sore am I and ill,
    If I stand stock still;
    I eat not a nedyll[120]
        This month and more.
1ST SHEPHERD. How fares thy wife? By my hood, how fares she?
MAC. Lies weltering! by the rood! by the fire, lo!
    And a house full of brood,[121] she drinks well too,
    Ill speed other good that she will do;
        But so
    Eats as fast as she can,
    And each year that comes to man,
    She brings forth a lakan,[122]
        And some years two.
    But were I not more gracious, and richer by far,
    I were eaten out of house, and of harbour,
    Yet is she a foul dowse, if ye come near.
    There is none that trows, nor knows, a war[123]
        Than ken I.
    Now will ye see what I proffer,
    To give all in my coffer

---

[116] eye.
[117] jest.
[118] rumour (ill repute).
[119] hot.
[120] needle—not a little bit.
[121] brood, children.
[122] plaything.
[123] worse.

To-morrow next to offer,
    Her head mass-penný.
2ND SHEPHERD. I wot so forwaked[124] is none in this shire:
    I would sleep if I taked less to my hire.
3RD SHEPHERD. I am cold and naked, and would have a fire.
1ST SHEPHERD. I am weary for-raked,[125] and run in the mire.
    Wake thou!
2ND SHEPHERD. Nay, I will lie down-by,
    For I must sleep truly.
3RD SHEPHERD. As good a man's son was I
    As any of you.
    But, Mac, come hither, between us shalt thou lie.
MAC. Then might I stay you bedene:[126] of that ye would say,—
    No dread.
    From my head to my toe
    Mantis tuas commendo,
    Pontio Pilato.[127]
        Christ's cross me speed,

[*He rises, the shepherds sleeping, and says:*]

Now were time for a man, that lacks what he wold,
To stalk privately then into a fold,
And namely to work then, and be not too bold,
He might abide the bargain, if it were told
    At the ending.
Now were time for to revel;
But he needs good counsel
That fain would fare well,
    And has but little spending.

[MAC *works a spell on them.*]

But about you a circle, as round as a moon,
Till I have done that I will, till that it be noon,
That ye lie stone-still, till that I have done,
And I shall say there till of good words a foyn[128]
    On height;
Over your heads my hand I lift,
Out go your eyes, fore to do your sight,

---

[124] early waked, or perhaps, wearied by watching.
[125] over-walked.
[126] at once.
[127] Into thy hands I commend (them), Pontius Pilate.
[128] few.

But yet I must make better shift,
    And it be right.
What, Lord? they sleep hard! that may ye all hear;
Was I never a shepherd, but now will I leer[129]
If the flock be scared, yet shall I nap near,
Who draws hitherward, now mends our cheer,
    From sorrow:
A fat sheep I dare say,
A good fleece dare I lay,
Eft white when I may,
    But this will I borrow.

[*He steals a sheep and goes home.*]

MAC. [*at his own door.*] How, Gill, art thou in? Get us some light.
HIS WIFE. Who makes such din this time of night?
    I am set for to spin: I hope not I might
    Rise a penny to win: I shrew them on height.
        So fares
    A housewife that has been
    To be raised thus between:
    There may no note be seen
        For such small chares.[130]
MAC. Good wife, open the hek.[131] See'st thou not what I bring?
WIFE. I may let thee draw the sneck. Ah! come in, my sweeting.
MAC. Yea, thou dost not reck of my long standing.
WIFE. By thy naked neck, thou art like for to hang.
MAC. Go away:
    I am worthy of my meat,
    For in a strait can I get
    More than they that swinck[132] and sweat
        All the long day,
    Thus it fell to my lot, Gill, I had such grace.
WIFE. It were a foul blot to be hanged for the case.
MAC. I have scaped, Jelott, oft as hard as glass.
WIFE. "But so long goes the pot to the water," men says,
    "At last comes it home broken."
MAC. Well know I the token,
    But let it never be spoken;
        But come and help fast.
    I would he were flayn;[133] I list we'll eat:

---

[129] learn.
[130] chare,—job, as in charwoman.
[131] wicket.
[132] toil.

This twelvemonth was I not so fain of one sheep-meat.
WIFE. Come they if he be slain, and hear the sheep bleat?
MAC. Then might I be ta'en: that were a cold sweat.
    Go bar
      The gate door.
WIFE. Yes, Mac,
    For and they come at thy back.
MAC. Then might I pay for all the pack:
    The devil of them war![134]
WIFE. A good bowrde[135] have I spied, since thou can none:
    Here shall we him hide, till they be gone;
    In my cradle abide. Let me alone,
    And I shall lie beside in childbed and groan.
MAC. Thou red?[136]
    And I shall say thou wast light
    Of a knave child this night.
WIFE. Now well is my day bright,
      That ever I was bred.
    This is a good guise and a far cast;
    Yet a woman's advice helps at the last.
    I care never who spies: again go thou fast.
MAC. But I come or they rise; else blows a cold blast—
    I will go sleep.

[MAC *goes back to the field.*]

    Yet sleep all this menye,[137]
    And I shall go stalk privily,
    As it had never been I
      That carried their sheep.
1ST SHEPHERD. Resurrex à mortrius: have hold my hand.
    Judas carnas dominus, I may not well stand:
    My foot sleeps, by Jesus, and I water fastand!
    I thought that we laid us full near England.
2ND SHEPHERD. Ah ye!
    Lord, how I have slept weel!
    As fresh as an eel,
      As light I me feel
      As leaf on a tree.
3RD SHEPHERD. Benste![138] be herein! So my head quakes

---

[133] flayed.
[134] The devil of them give warning.
[135] jest.
[136] advisest, sayest so?
[137] company.

My heart is out of skin, what so it makes.
Who makes all this din? So my brow aches,
To the door will I win. Hark fellows, wakes!
    We were four:
See ye anything of Mac now?
1ST SHEPHERD. We were up ere thou.
2ND SHEPHERD. Man, I give God a vow,
    Yet heed he nowhere.
3RD SHEPHERD. Methought he was wrapped in a wolf's-skin.
1ST SHEPHERD. So are many happed, now namely within.
2ND SHEPHERD. When we had long napped; methought with a gin
    A fat sheep he trapped, but he made no din.
3RD SHEPHERD. Be still:
    Thy dream makes thee wood:[139]
    It is but phantom, by the rood.
1ST SHEPHERD. Now God turn all to good,
    If it be his will.
2ND SHEPHERD. Rise, Mac, for shame! thou ly'st right long.
MAC. Now Christ, his holy name be us amang,
    What is this? for Saint James!—I may not well gang.
    I trust I be the same. Ah! my neck has lain wrang
        Enough
    Mickle thank, since yester-even
    Now, by Saint Stephen!
    I was flayed with a sweven,—[140]
        My heart out of slough.[141]
    I thought Gill began to croak, and travail full sad,
    Well nigh at the first cock,—of a young lad,
    For to mend our flock: then be I never glad.
    To have two on my rock,—more than ever I had.
        Ah, my head!
    A house full of young tharmes,[142]
    The devil knock out their harnes![143]
    Woe is he has many bairns,
        And thereto little bread.
    I must go home, by your leave, to Gill as I thought.
    I pray you look my sleeve, that I steal nought:
    I am loth you to grieve, or from you take aught.
3RD SHEPHERD. Go forth, ill might thou chefe,[144] now would I we

---

[138] Benedicite.
[139] mad
[140] dream.
[141] sloth
[142] bellies.
[143] brains.

sought,
>This morn,
>That we had all our store.

1ST SHEPHERD. But I will go before,
>Let us meet.

2ND SHEPHERD. Whor?[145]

3RD SHEPHERD. At the crooked thorn.

MAC. [*at his own door again.*] Undo this door! who is here? How long
shall I stand?

WIFE. Who makes such a stir?—Now walk in the wenyand.[146]

MAC. Ah, Gill, what cheer?—It is I, Mac, your husband.

HIS WIFE. Then may we be here,—the devil in a band,
>>Sir Gile.
>Lo, he commys[147] with a lot,
>As he were holden in the throat.
>I may not sit, work or not
>>A hand long while.

MAC. Will ye hear what fare she makes—to get her a glose,[148]
>And do naught but lakes[149]—and close her toes.

WIFE. Why, who wanders, who wakes,—who comes, who goes?
>Who brews, who bakes? Who makes for me this hose?
>>And then
>It is ruth to behold,
>Now in hot, now in cold,
>Full woful is the household
>>That wants a woman.
>But what end hast thou made with the herds, Mac?

MAC. The last word that they said,—when I turned my back,
>They would look that they had—their sheep all the pack.
>I hope they will not be well paid,—when they their sheep lack.
>>Perdie!
>But howso the game goes,
>To me they will suppose,
>And make a foul noise,
>>And cry out upon me.
>But thou must do as thou hight,

WIFE. I accord me thertylle.[150]
>I shall swaddle him right in my cradle.

---

[144] prosper.
[145] where.
[146] waning moon.
[147] comes.
[148] lie.
[149] plays.
[150] thereto.

If it were a greater slight, yet could I help till.
I will lie down straight. Come hap me.
MAC. I will.
WIFE. Behind,
   Come Coll and his marrow,
   They will nip us full narrow.
MAC. But I may cry out "Harro!"[151]
   The sheep if they find.
WIFE. Hearken aye when they call: they will come anon.
   Come and make ready all, and sing by thine own,
   Sing "Lullay!" thou shall, for I must groan,
   And cry out by the wall on Mary and John,
      For sore.
   Sing "Lullay" full fast
   When thou hears at the last;
   And but I play a false cast
      Trust me no more.

[*Re-enter the* THREE SHEPHERDS.]

3RD SHEPHERD. Ah, Coll! good morn:—why sleepest thou not?
1ST SHEPHERD. Alas, that ever was I born!—we have a foul blot.
   A fat wether have we lorne.[152]
3RD SHEPHERD. Marry, Godys forbot![153]
2ND SHEPHERD. Who should do us that scorn? That were a foul spot.
1ST SHEPHERD. Some shrew.
   I have sought with my dogs,
   All Horbery shrogs,[154]
   And of fifteen hogs
      Found I but one ewe.
3RD SHEPHERD. Now trust me if you will;—by Saint Thomas of Kent!
   Either Mac or Gill—was at that assent.
1ST SHEPHERD. Peace, man, be still;—I saw when he went.
   Thou slander'st him ill; thou ought to repent.
      Good speed.
2ND SHEPHERD. Now as ever might I thee,
   If I should even here dee,[155]
   I would say it were he,
      That did that same deed.
3RD SHEPHERD. Go we thither I rede,[156]—and run on our feet.

---

[151] Help! or Halloo!
[152] lost.
[153] God forbid.
[154] Horbery Shrubberies, near Wakefield.
[155] die.

May I never eat bread,—the truth till I wit.

1ST SHEPHERD. Nor drink, in my heed,—with him till I meet.

2ND SHEPHERD. I will rest in no stead, till that I him greet,
 My brother
One I will hight:[157]
Till I see him in sight
Shall I never sleep one night
 There I do another.

3RD SHEPHERD. Will ye hear how they hack,[158]—Our Sire! list, how they croon!

1ST SHEPHERD. Hard I never none crack,—so clear out of tune.
 Call on him.

2ND SHEPHERD. Mac! undo your door soon.

MAC. Who is it that spoke,—as it were noon?
 On loft,
Who is that I say?

3RD SHEPHERD. Good fellows! were it day?

MAC. As far as ye may,—
 Good, speak ye soft!
Over a sick woman's head,—that is ill mate ease,
I had liefer be dead,—or she had any disease.

WIFE. Go to another stead; I may not well queasse[159]
Each foot that ye tread—goes near make me sneeze[160]
 So he!

1ST SHEPHERD. Tell us, Mac, if ye may,
 How fare ye, I say?

MAC. But are ye in this town to-day?
 Now how fare ye?
Ye have run in the mire, and are wet yit:
I shall make you a fire, if ye will sit.
A horse would I hire; think ye on it.
Well quit is my hire, my dream—this is it.
 A season.
I have bairns if ye knew,
Well more than enew,[161]
But we must drink as we brew,
 And that is but reason.
I would ye dined e'er ye yode:[162] methink that ye sweat.

---

[156] advise.
[157] call.
[158] "take on," make game.
[159] breathe.
[160] nose (?) The "so he" is meant for a she.
[161] enow, enough.
[162] went.

2ND SHEPHERD. Nay, neither mends our mode, drink nor meat.
MAC. Why, sir, ails you aught, but good?
3RD SHEPHERD. Yes, our sheep that we gat,
    Are stolen as they yode.[163] Our loss is great.
MAC. Sirs, drinkýs!
    Had I been there,
    Some should have bought it full dear.
1ST SHEPHERD. Marry, some men trows that ye were,
      And that us forethinkýs.[164]
2ND SHEPHERD. Mac, some men trows that it should be ye.
3RD SHEPHERD. Either ye or your spouse; so say we.
MAC. Now if ye have suspouse[165] to Gill or to me,
    Come and rip our house, and then may ye see
      Who had her.
    If I any sheep got,
    Either cow or stot,
    And Gill, my wife rose not
      Here since she laid her.
    As I am both true and leal, to God here I pray,
    That this be the first meal, I shall eat this day.
1ST SHEPHERD. Mac, as I have weal, arise thee, I say!
    "He learned timely to steal, that could not say nay."
WIFE. I swelt.[166]
    Out thieves from my once!
      Ye come to rob us for the nonce.
MAC. Hear ye not how she groans?
      Your heart should melt.
WIFE. Out thieves, from my bairn! Nigh him not thore.
MAC. Knew ye how she had farne,[167] your hearts would be sore.
    Ye do wrong, I you warn, that thus commys before
    To a woman that has farn;[168] but I say no more.
WIFE. Ah, my middle!
    I pray to God so mild,
    If ever I you beguiled,
    That I eat this child,
      That lies in this cradle.
MAC. Peace, woman, for God's pain, and cry not so:
    Thou spill'st thy brain, and mak'st me full woe.
2ND SHEPHERD. I know our sheep be slain, what find ye too?

---

[163] went, were grazing.
[164] bothers us, makes us suspect.
[165] suspicion.
[166] swelter.
[167] fared.
[168] been in labour.

3RD SHEPHERD. All work we in vain: as well may we go.
　　But hatters.[169]
　　I can find no flesh,
　　Hard nor nesh,[170]
　　Salt nor fresh,
　　　But two tome[171] platters:
　　No cattle but this, tame nor wild,
　　None, as have I bliss; as loud as he smiled.
WIFE. No, so God me bliss, and give me joy of my child.
1ST SHEPHERD. We have markëd amiss: I hold us beguiled.
2ND SHEPHERD. Sir, done!
　　Sir, our lady him save,
　　Is your child a knave?[172]
MAC. Any lord might him have
　　This child to his son.
　　When he wakens he skips, that joy is to see.
3RD SHEPHERD. In good time, be his steps, and happy they be!
　　But who was his gossips, tell now to me!
MAC. So fair fall their lips!
1ST SHEPHERD. [*aside.*] Hark now, a lee![173]
MAC. So God them thank,
　　Parkin, and Gibbon Waller, I say,
　　And gentle John Horne, in good fay,[174]
　　He made all the garray,[175]
　　　With the great shank.
2ND SHEPHERD. Mac, friends will we be, for we are all one.
MAC. Why! now I hold for me, for help get I none.
　　Farewell all three: all glad were ye gone.
3RD SHEPHERD. Fair words may there be, but love there is none.
1ST SHEPHERD. Gave ye the child anything?
2ND SHEPHERD. I trust not one farthing.
3RD SHEPHERD. Fast again will I fling,
　　Abide ye me there. [*He returns to* MAC'S *cot.*]
　　Mac, take it to no grief, if I come to thy barn.
MAC. Nay, thou dost me great reprieve, and foul hast thou farne.[176]
3RD SHEPHERD. The child will it not grieve, that little day starn.[177]
　　Mac, with your leave, let me give your bairn,

---

[169] confound it.
[170] soft.
[171] empty.
[172] a boy.
[173] a lie.
[174] faith.
[175] hubbub.
[176] done.
[177] day-star.

But sixpence.

MAC. Nay, go 'way: he sleepys.

3RD SHEPHERD. Methink he peepys.

MAC. When he wakens he weepys.

I pray you go hence.

3RD SHEPHERD. Give me leave him to kiss, and lift up the clout.

What the devil is this? He has a long snout.

1ST SHEPHERD. He is marked amiss. We wait ill about.

2ND SHEPHERD. Ill spun weft, I wis, aye cometh foul out;

Aye so;

He is like to our sheep.

3RD SHEPHERD. How, Gib, may I peep?

1ST SHEPHERD. I trow, kind will creep,

Where it may not go.

2ND SHEPHERD. This was a quaint gaud,[178] and a far cast

It was a high fraud.

3RD SHEPHERD. Yea, sirs, was't.

Let burn this bawd and bind her fast.

A false skawd[179] hangs at the last;

So shall thou.

Will ye see how they swaddle

His four feet in the middle?

Saw I never in a cradle

A hornëd lad e'er now.

MAC. Peace bid I: what! let be your fare;

I am he that him gat, and yond woman him bare.

1ST SHEPHERD. What devil shall he halt?[180] Mac, lo, God makes air.

2ND SHEPHERD. Let be all that. Now God give him care!

I sagh.[181]

WIFE. A pretty child is he,

As sits upon a woman's knee;

A dylly-downe, perdie!

To make a man laugh.

3RD SHEPHERD. I know him by the ear mark:—that is a good token.

MAC. I tell you, sirs, hark:—his nose was broken.

Since then, told me a clerk,—that he was forespoken.[182]

1ST SHEPHERD. This is a false work.—I would fain be wroken:[183]

Get a weapon!

WIFE. He was taken by an elf;[184]

---

[178] gem, something prankt out, or shown off, like a false gem.

[179] scold

[180] hight, be called.

[181] say

[182] bewitched

[183] be avenged, wreak vengeance.

I saw it myself.
When the clock struck twelve,
   Was he mis-shapen.
2ND SHEPHERD. Ye two are right deft,—same in a stead.
3RD SHEPHERD. Since they maintain their theft,—let's do them to dead.
MAC. If I trespass eft, gird off my head.
   With you will I be left.
1ST SHEPHERD. Sirs, do my red
   For this trespass,
We will neither ban nor flyte[185]
Fight, nor chyte,[186]
But seize him tight,
   And cast him in canvas.

[*They toss* MAC *for his sins.*]

[1ST SHEPHERD *as the three return to the fold.*]

Lord, how I am sore, in point for to tryst:
In faith I may no more, therefore will I rest.
2ND SHEPHERD. As a sheep of seven score, he weighed in my fist.
   For to sleep anywhere, methink that I list.
3RD SHEPHERD. Now I pray you,
   Lie down on this green.
1ST SHEPHERD. On these thefts yet I mean.
3RD SHEPHERD. Whereto should ye tene?[187]
   Do as I say you.

[*Enter an* ANGEL *above, who sings "Gloria in Excelsis," then says:*]

Rise, hired-men, heynd,[188] for now is he born
That shall take from the fiend, that Adam had lorn:[189]
That warlock to sheynd,[190] this night is he born.
God is made your friend: now at this morn,
   He behests;
To Bedlem go see,
There lies that free[191]

---

[184] i.e. for a changeling.
[185] curse nor flout.
[186] chide.
[187] vex about it.
[188] gracious.
[189] lost.
[190] destroy.
[191] free, or divine, One.

In a crib full poorly,
Betwixt two beasts.

1ST SHEPHERD. This was a quaint stevyn[192] that ever yet I heard.
It is a marvel to nevyn[193] thus to be scared.

2ND SHEPHERD. Of God's son of heaven, he spoke up word.
All the wood like the levin,[194] methought that he gard
Appear.

3RD SHEPHERD. He spoke of a bairn
In Bedlem I you warn.

1ST SHEPHERD. That betokens yonder starn[195]
Let us seek him there.

2ND SHEPHERD. Say, what was his song? Heard ye not how he cracked it?
Three breves to a long.[196]

3RD SHEPHERD. Yea, marry, he hacked[197] it.
Was no crochet wrong, nor no thing that lacked it.

1ST SHEPHERD. For to sing us among, right as he knacked it,
I can.

2ND SHEPHERD. Let us see how ye croon
Can ye bark at the moon?

3RD SHEPHERD. Hold your tongues, have done.

1ST SHEPHERD. Hark after, then.

2ND SHEPHERD. To Bedlem he bade—that we should gang:
I am full feared—that we tarry too lang.

3RD SHEPHERD. Be merry and not sad: of mirth is our sang,
Everlasting glad, our road may we fang,[198]
Without noise.

1ST SHEPHERD. Hie we thither quickly;
If we be wet and weary,
To that child and that lady
We have it not to slose.[199]

2ND SHEPHERD. We find by the prophecy—let be your din—
Of David and Esai, and more than I min;[200]
They prophesied by clergy, that on a virgin
Should he light and ly, to pardon our sin
And slake it,
Our kind from woe;

---

[192] voice.
[193] name, relate.
[194] lightning.
[195] star.
[196] three short notes to a long one.
[197] shouted it out.
[198] take.
[199] delay.
[200] can mind.

For Esai said so,
  Cite virgo
  Concipiet a child that is naked.
3RD SHEPHERD. Full glad may we be,—and abide that day
  That lovely to see,—that all mights may.
  Lord, well for me,—for once and for aye,
  Might I kneel on my knee—some word for to say
    To that child.
  But the angel said
  In a crib was he laid;
  He was poorly arrayed,
    Both meaner and mild.
1ST SHEPHERD. Patriarchs that have been,—and prophets beforn,
  They desired to have seen—this child that is born.
  They are gone full clean,—that have they lorn.
  We shall see him, I ween,—e'er it be morn
    By token
  When I see him and feel,
  Then know I full weel
  It is true as steel
    That prophets have spoken.
  To so poor as we are, that he would appear,
  First find, and declare by his messenger.
2ND SHEPHERD. Go we now, let us fare: the place is us near.
3RD SHEPHERD. I am ready and yare:[201] go we in fear
    To that light!
  Lord! if thy wills be,
  We are lewd[202] all three,
  Thou grant us of thy glee,[203]
    To comfort thy wight.

[*The* SHEPHERDS *arrive at Bethlehem.*]

1ST SHEPHERD. Hail, comely and clean; hail, young child!
  Hail, maker, as I mean, of a maiden so mild!
  Thou hast wared, I ween, off the warlock[204] so wild,
  The false guiler of teen,[205] now goes he beguiled.
    Lo, he merry is!
  Lo, he laughs, my sweeting,
  A welcome meeting!

---

[201] eager.
[202] unlearn'd, rude.
[203] happiness.
[204] demon, evil one.
[205] worker of evil. The "he" in the next line refers to the Holy Babe again.

>   I have given my greeting
>   Have a bob of cherries?

2ND SHEPHERD. Hail, sovereign saviour, for thou hast us sought!
> Hail freely, leaf and flow'r, that all thing has wrought!
> Hail full of favour, that made all of nought!
> Hail! I kneel and I cower. A bird have I brought
>   To my bairn!
> Hail, little tiny mop,[206]
> Of our creed thou are crop!
> I would drink in thy cup,
>   Little day-starn.[207]

3RD SHEPHERD. Hail, darling dear, full of godheed!
> I pray thee be near, when that I have need.
> Hail! sweet is thy cheer: my heart would bleed
> To see thee sit here in so poor weed.
>   With no pennies.
> Hail! put forth thy dall!—[208]
> I bring thee but a ball
> Have and play thee with all,
>   And go to the tennis.

MARY. The Father of Heaven, God omnipotent,
> That set all on levin,[209] his son has he sent.
> My name could he neven,[210] and laught as he went.[211]
> I conceived him full even, through might, as God meant;
>   And new is he born.
> He keep you from woe:
> I shall pray him so;
> Tell forth as ye go,
>   And mind on this morn.

1ST SHEPHERD. Farewell, lady, so fair to behold,
> With thy child on thy knee.

2ND SHEPHERD. But he lies full cold,
> Lord, well is me: now we go forth, behold!

3RD SHEPHERD. Forsooth, already it seems to be told
>   Full oft.

1ST SHEPHERD. What grace we have fun.[212]

2ND SHEPHERD. Come forth, now are we won.

3RD SHEPHERD. To sing are we bun:[213]

---

[206] pate, little tiny-pate

[207] day-star.

[208] hand.

[209] set all alight; gave light to all.

[210] could he (i.e. the babe) tell, name.

[211] weened; i.e. laughed as if he knew all about it.

[212] found.

Let take on loft.[214]

---

[213] bound.
[214] Let us sing it aloft, or aloud!

The Coventry Nativity Play

CHARACTERS

ISAIAH (AS PROLOGUE)
GABRIEL
JOSEPH
MARY
THE THREE KINGS
THE THREE SHEPHERDS
THE TWO PROPHETS
KING HEROD
A HERALD
AN ANGEL
TWO SOLDIERS
THREE WOMEN

THE COVENTRY NATIVITY PLAY OF THE COMPANY OF SHEARMEN AND TAILORS

PROLOGUE

ISAIAH. The sovereign that seeth every secret
　　　He save you all and make you perfect and strong:
　　　And give his grace with his mercy thereto meet,
　　　For now in great misery mankind is bound.
　　　The serpent hath given us so mortal a wound
　　　That no creature is able us for to release
　　　Till the right unction of Judah doth cease.
　　　　Then shall much mirth and joy increase
　　　And the right root in Israel spring,
　　　That shall bring forth the grain of holiness:
　　　And out of danger he shall us bring
　　　Into that region where he is king:
　　　Which above all other doth abound
　　　And that cruel Satan he shall confound.
　　　　Wherefore I come here upon this ground,
　　　To comfort every creature of birth;
　　　For I, Isaiah, the prophet, hath found
　　　Many sweet matters, whereof we may make mirth
　　　On this same wise.
　　　For though Adam be doomed to death
　　　With all his children, as Abel and Seth:

Yet, Ecce virgo concipiet![215]
Lo, where a remedy shall rise!
  Behold a maid shall conceive a child,
And get us more grace than ever man had.
And her maidenhood nothing defiled:
She is deputed to bear the Son, Almighty God.
Lo, sovereignties now may you be glad,
For of this maiden all we may be fain;[216]
For Adam that now lies in sorrows full sad,
Her glorious birth shall redeem him again
From bondage and thrall.
Now be merry every man,
For this deed briefly in Israel shall be done,
And before the Father on his throne
That shall glad us all.
  More of this matter fain would I move,
But longer time I have not here for to dwell.
That lord that is merciful, his mercy so in us may prove
For to save our souls from the darkness of hell,
  And to his bliss—he us bring
  As he is—both lord and king;
  And shall be everlasting
  In secula seculos:[217] Amen. [*Exit.*]

[*Enter* GABRIEL *to* MARY.]

GABRIEL. Hail! Mary, full of grace,
  Our Lord God is with thee!
  Above all women that ever was;
  Lady, blessed may thou be.
MARY. Almighty Father and King of bliss
  From all dyskes[218] thou save me now:
  For inwardly my spirit troubled is,
  I am amazed and know not how.
GABRIEL. Dread thee nothing, maiden, of this:
  From heaven above hither am I sent,
  Of embassage from that King of bliss,
  Unto the lady and virgin reverent,
  Saluting thee here as most excellent,
  Whose virtue above all other doth abound;
  Wherefore in thee grace shall be found:

---

[215] "Behold, a Virgin shall conceive!"
[216] glad.
[217] for ever and ever.
[218] deceits, darknesses.

For thou shalt conceive upon this ground
The Second Person of God on throne;
He will be born of thee alone,
Without sin tho shalt him see.
Thy grace and thy goodness will never be gone
But ever to live in virginity.

MARY. I marvel sore how that may be:
Man's company knew I never yet,
Nor never to do cast I me,
While that our Lord sendeth me my wit.

GABRIEL. The Holy Ghost in thee shall light,
And shall endue thy soul so with virtue
From the Father that is on high:
These words, turtle, they be full true.

This child that of thee shall be born
Is the Second Person in Trinity.
He shall save that was forlorn,
And the fiend's power destroy shall he.

These words, lady, full true they be,
And further, lady, in thy own lineage,
Behold Elizabeth, thy cousin clean,
The which was barren and past all age.

And now with child she hath been
Six months and more as shall be seen;
Wherefore, discomfort thee not, Mary,
For to God impossible nothing may be.

MARY. Now and it be that Lord's will
Of my body to be born and for to be
His high pleasure for to fulfil,
As his one handmaid I submit me.

GABRIEL. Now blessed be the time set
That thou wast born in thy degree:
For now is the knot surely knit
And God conceived in Trinity.

Now farewell lady of might most,
Unto the Godhead I thee beteyche.[219]

MARY. That lord thee guide in every cost
And lowly he lead me and be my leech.[220]

[*Here the* ANGEL *departeth and* JOSEPH *cometh in and saith:*]

---

[219] commit.
[220] physician, healer.

JOSEPH. Mary, my wife so dear!
　　How do ye, dame, and what cheer
　　Is with you this tide?
MARY. Truly, husband, I am here
　　Our Lord's will for to abide.
JOSEPH. What! I trow we be all shent![221]
　　Say, woman, who hath been here since I went
　　To rage with thee?
MARY. Sir, here was neither man, nor man's even,[222]
　　But only the sond[223] of our Lord God in heaven.
JOSEPH. Say not so, woman, for shame let be:
　　Ye be with child so wondrous great,
　　Ye need no more thereof to treat
　　Against all right.
　　For sooth this child, dame, is not mine;
　　Alas, that ever with my eyne[224]
　　I should see this sight.
　　Tell me, woman, whose is this child?
MARY. None but yours, husband, so mild
　　And that shall be seen, I wis.
JOSEPH. But mine, alas! alas! why say ye so?
　　Well away, woman, now may I go
　　Beguiled as many another is.
MARY. Nay truly, sir, ye be not beguiled
　　Nor yet with spot of sin I am not defiled;
　　Trust it well, husband.
JOSEPH. Husband in faith, and that acold;
　　Ah well away, Joseph, as thou art old!
　　Like a fool now may I stand
　　And truss; but in faith, Mary, thou art in sin.
　　So much as I have cherished thee, dame, and all thy kin,
　　Behind my back to serve me thus:
　　　All old men example take by me,
　　How I am beguiled here may you see,
　　To wed so young a child.
　　Now farewell, Mary, I leave thee here alone,
　　Woe worth thee dame, and thy works each one!
　　For I will no more be beguiled
　　For friend nor foe.
　　Now of this deed I am so dull
　　And of my life I am so full,

---

[221] ruined.
[222] equal or like.
[223] messenger.
[224] eyes.

No farther may I go.

ANGEL. Arise up, Joseph, and go home again
    Unto Mary thy wife that is so free;
    To comfort her look that thou be fain,
    For, Joseph, a clean maiden is she.
    She hath conceived without any trayne
    The Second Person in Trinity:
    Jesu shall be his name certainly,
    And all this world save shall he.
    Be not aghast.

JOSEPH. Now, Lord, I thank thee with heart full sad.
    For of these tidings I am so glad
    That all my care away is cast,
    Wherefore to Mary I will in haste.
      Ah, Mary, Mary, I kneel full low,
    Forgive me, sweet wife, here in this land;
    Mercy, Mary, for now I know
    Of your good governance and how it doth stand:
    Though that I did thee misname.
    Mercy, Mary, while I live
    Will I never, sweet wife, thee grieve,
    In earnest nor in game.

MARY. Now, that Lord in Heaven, sir,—he you forgive!
    And I do forgive you in his name
    For evermore.

JOSEPH. Now truly, sweet wife, to you I say the same;
    But now to Bethlehem must I wynde[225]
    And show myself so full of care,
    And I to leave you this great behind,
    God wot, the while, dame, how you should fare.

MARY. Nay hardily, husband, dread ye nothing,
    For I will walk with you on the way.
    I trust in God, Almighty King,
    To speed right well in our journey.

JOSEPH. Now I thank you, Mary, of your goodness
    That you my words will not blame;
    And since that to Bethlehem we shall us address
    Go we together in God's holy name.

[*They set out on their way.*]

    Now to Bethlehem have we leagues three,
    The day is nigh spent, it draweth towards night,

---

[225] wend, journey.

Fain at your ease, dame, I would that ye should be:
For you grow all weary, it seemeth, in my sight.
MARY. God have mercy, Joseph, my spouse, so dear!
All prophets hereto do bear witness
The evry time now draweth near
That my child will be born, which is King of bliss.
Unto some place, Joseph, kindly me lead,
That I might rest me with grace in this tide,
The light of the Father over us both spread
And the grace of my son with us here abide.
JOSEPH. Lo, blessed Mary, here shall ye lend;[226]
Chief chosen of our Lord, and cleanest in degree:
And I for help to town, will I wend.
Is not this the best, dame, what say ye?
MARY. God have mercy! Joseph, my husband, so meek,
And I heartily pray you go now from me.
JOSEPH. That shall be done in haste, Mary, so sweet!
The comfort of the Holy Ghost leave I with thee.
Now to Bethlehem strait will I go,
To get some help for Mary so free,
Some help of women, God may me send!
That Mary, full of grace, pleased may be.

[*Enter a* SHEPHERD.]

1ST SHEPHERD. Now God that art in Trinity,
Thou sawest my fellows and me;
For I know not where my sheep nor they be,
This night it is so cold,
Now is it nigh the middest of the night,
These weathers are dark and dim of light,
That of them can I have no sight,
Standing here on this wold.
But now to make their hearts light,
Now will I full right
Stand upon this loe.[227]
And to them cry with all my might:
Full well my voice they know,
What ho, fellows, ho, hoo, ho!

[*Enter two other* SHEPHERDS.]

---

[226] stay.
[227] hill.

2ND SHEPHERD. Hark, Sym, hark, I hear our brother on the loe,[228]
    This is his voice, right well I know,
    Therefore towards him let us go,
    And follow his voice aright,
    See, Sym, see where he doth stand;
    I am right glad we have him found.
    Brother! where hast thou been so long,
    And it is so cold this night?
1ST SHEPHERD. Oh, friends! there came a pyrie[228] of wind
    With a mist suddenly,
    That forth off my ways went I,
    And great heaviness then made I,
    And was full sore afright;
    Then for to go wist I not whither,
    But travelled on this hill hither and thither.
    I was so weary of this cold weather,
    That near passed was my might.
3RD SHEPHERD. Brother, now we be past that fright,
    And it is far within the night:
    Full soon will spring the daylight,
    It draweth full near the tide.
    Here awhile let us rest
    And repast ourselves of the best.
    Till that the sun rise in the east,
    Let us all here abide.

    [*There the* SHEPHERDS *draw forth their meat, and do eat and drink,
       and as they drink they see the star and say thus:*]

    Brother, look up and behold,
    What thing is yonder that shineth so bright?
    As long as ever I have watched my fold,
    Yet saw I never such a sight
    In field.
    Aha! now is come the time that old fathers hath told,
    That in the winter's night so cold,
    A child of maiden born, be he would,
    In whom all prophecies shall be fulfilled.
1ST SHEPHERD. Truth it is without nay,
    So said the prophet Isaye,
    That a child should be born of a maid so bright
    In winter nigh the shortest day,

---

[228] gust.

Or else in the middest of the night.
2ND SHEPHERD. Loved be God, most of might!
That our grace is to see that sight;
Pray we to him as it is right
If that his will it be,
That we may have knowledge of this signification,
And why it appeareth on this fashion
And ever to him let us give laudation,
In earth, while that we be.

[*There the* ANGELS *sing "Gloria in Excelsis Deo."*]

3RD SHEPHERD. Hark, they sing above in the clouds clear!
Heard I never of so merry a choir.
Now gentle brother draw we near
To hear their harmony?
1ST SHEPHERD. Brother, mirth and solace is come us among
For, by the sweetness of their song;
God's Son is come, whom we have looked for long,
As signifieth this star we do see.
2ND SHEPHERD. Glory, Gloria in Excelsis, that was their song,
How say ye fellows! said they not thus?
1ST SHEPHERD. That is well said, now go we hence
To worship that child of high magnificence;
And that we may sing in his presence,
Et in terra pax omnibus.

[*There the* SHEPHERDS *sing:*]

As I out rode this enderes' night,
Of three jolly shepherds I saw a sight,
And all about their fold a star shone bright;
They sang, Terli, terlow;
So merrily the shepherds their pipes can blow.
JOSEPH. Now, Lord, this noise that I do hear
With this great solemnity,
Greatly amended hath my cheer,
I trust high news shortly will be.

[*There the* ANGELS *sing "Gloria in Excelsis" again.*]

MARY. Ah Joseph, husband, come hither anon
My child is born that is King of bliss.
JOSEPH. Now welcome to me, the maker of man,
With all the homage that I can;

Thy sweet mother here will I kiss.

MARY. Ah Joseph, husband, my child waxeth cold
    And we have no fire to warm him with.

JOSEPH. Now in my arms I shall him fold,
    King of all kings by field and by frith,[229]
    He might have had better, and himself would
    Than the breathing of these beasts to warm him with.

MARY. Now, Joseph, my husband, fetch hither my child,
    The maker of man, and high King of bliss.

JOSEPH. That shall be done, anon, Mary so mild!
    For the breathing of these beasts hath warmed him, I wis.

1ST ANGEL. Herdmen kind, dread ye nothing,
    Of this star that ye do see;
    For this same morn God's son is born,
    In Bethlem of a maiden fre.[230]

2ND ANGEL. Hie you hither in haste,
    It is his will ye shall him see
    Lying in a crib of poor repast;
    Yet of David's line come is he.

1ST SHEPHERD. Hail, maid-mother, and wife so mild!
    As the angel said, so have we found,
    I have nothing to present to thy child,
    But my pipe; hold, hold! take it in thy hand;
    Wherein much pleasure that I have found,
    And now to honour thy glorious birth,
    Thou shalt it have to make thee mirth.

2ND SHEPHERD. Now, hail be thou, child, and thy dame,
    For in a poor lodging here art thou laid;
    So the angel said, and told us thy name.
    Hold, take thou here my hat on thy head,
    And now of one thing thou art well sped;
    For weather thou hast no cause to complain,
    For wind, nor sun, hail, snow, and rain.

3RD SHEPHERD. Hail, be thou Lord over water and lands
    For thy coming all we may make mirth,
    Have here my mittens to put on thy hands
    Other treasure have I none to present thee with.

MARY. Now, herdmen kind,
    For your coming,
    To my child shall I pray,
    As he is heaven's king,
    To grant you his blessing,

---

[229] wold.
[230] noble.

And to his bliss that ye may wynd[231]
At your last day.

[*There the* SHEPHERDS *sing again:*]

   Down from heaven, from heaven so high,
  Of angels there came a great company,
  With mirth, and joy, and great solemnity
  They sang, Terli, terlow;
  So merrily the shepherds their pipes can blow.

[*The two* PROPHETS *come in.*]

1ST PROPHET. Novellis, novellis,[232] of wonderful marvellys,[233]
  Were high and sweet unto the hearing,
  As Scripture tellis, these strange novellis
  To you I bring.
2ND PROPHET. Now, heartily, sir, I desire to know,
  If it would please you for to show,
  Of what manner a thing?
1ST PROPHET. Were it mystical unto your hearing,—
  Of the nativity of a king?
2ND PROPHET. Of a king?
  Whence should he come?
1ST PROPHET. From that region royal and mighty mansion,
  The seed celestial and heavenly wisdom,
  The Second Person, and God's one Son,
  For our sake is man become.
  This godly sphere, descended here,
  Into a virgin clear,
  She undefiled,
  By whose work, obscure our frail nature
  Is now beguiled.
2ND PROPHET. Why, hath she a child?
1ST PROPHET. Ah, trust it well,
  And never the less,
  Yet is she a maid even as she was,
  And her son the king of Israel.
2ND PROPHET. A wonderful marvel, How that may be,
  And far doth excel—
    All our capacity,

---

[231] win.

[232] News, news!

[233] marvels.

How that the trinity,
   Of so high regality,
Should joined be,
   Unto our mortality.
1ST PROPHET. Of his one great mercy
   As ye shall see the exposition,
Through whose humanity all Adam's progeny
Redeemed shall be
   Out of perdition;
Sith man did offend, who should amend,
   But the said man and no other;
For the which cause he,
   Incarnate would be,
And live in misery
   As man's one brother.
2ND PROPHET. Sir, upon the Deity, I believe perfectly,
   Impossible to be, there is nothing;
Howbeit this work, unto me is dark,
   In the operation or working.
1ST PROPHET. What more reproof is unto belief
   Than to be doubting.
2ND PROPHET. Yet doubts ofttimes hath derivation.
1ST PROPHET. That is by the means of communication,
   Of truths to have a due probation,—
By the same doubts, reasoning.
2ND PROPHET. Then to you, this one thing,
   Of what noble and high lineage is she,
   That might this verible prince's mother be?
1ST PROPHET. Undoubted she is come of high parrage,[234]
   Of the house of David, and Solomon the sage,
   And one of the same line joined to her by marriage
Of whose tribe, we do subscribe
   This child's lineage.
2ND PROPHET. And why in that wise?
1ST PROPHET. For it was the guise
   To count the parent on the man's line,
   And not on the feminine,
Amongst us here in Israel.
2ND PROPHET. Yet can I not espy, by no wise
   How this child born should be without nature's prejudice.
1ST PROPHET. Nay, no prejudice unto nature I dare well say,
   For the king of nature may
   Have all his one will,

---

[234] descent, lineage.

Did not the power of God, make Aaron's rod
Bear fruit in one day?
2ND PROPHET. Truth it is indeed.
1ST PROPHET. Then look you and rede.[235]
2ND PROPHET. Ah! I perceive the seed
    Whereupon that you spake,
    It was for our need
    That he frail nature did take,
    And his blood he should shed
    Amends for to make
    For our transgression,
    As it is said in prophecy, that of the line of Judë
    Should spring a right Messië,
    By whom all we
    Should have redemption.
1ST PROPHET. Sir, now is the time come,
    And the date thereof run
    Of his Nativity.
2ND PROPHET. Yet I beseech you heartily,
    That ye would show me how
    That this strange novelty
    Were brought unto you?
1ST PROPHET. This other night so cold,
    Hereby upon a wold,
    Shepherds watching their fold
    In the night so far,
    To them appeared a star,
    And ever it drew them near,
    Which star they did behold,
    Brighter they say a thousand fold
    Than the sun so clear
    In his midday sphere;
    And they these tidings told.
2ND PROPHET. What, secretly?
1ST PROPHET. Na, na, hardily,[236]
    They made there of no council,
    For they sang as loud,
    As ever they could,
    Praising the king of Israel.
2ND PROPHET. Yet do I marvel,
    In what pile or castle,
    These herdmen did him see.

---

[235] give advice.
[236] boldly, openly.

1ST PROPHET. Neither in halls, nor yet in bowers,
  Born would he not be,
  Neither in castles, nor yet in towers,
  That seemly were to see,
  But at his Father's will,
  The prophecy to fulfil,
  Betwixt an ox and an ass
  Jesu this king born he was;
  Heaven he bring us till![237]
2ND PROPHET. Sir, ah! but when these shepherds had seen him there,
  To what place did they repair?
1ST PROPHET. Forth they went, and glad they were;
  Going they did sing,
  With mirth and solace, they made good cheer,
  For joy of that new tiding.
  And after as I heard them tell,
  He rewarded them full well
  He granted them heaven therein to dwell.
  In are they gone with joy and mirth,
  And their song it is Noël.

  [*There the* PROPHETS *go forth, and* HEROD *and the* MESSENGER *(or*
  HERALD*) comes in.*]

HERALD. Peace, Lord Barons of great renown!
  Peace, sir knights of noble presence!
  Peace, gentlemen companions of noble order!
  I command that all of you keep silence.
  Peace while your noble king is in presence!
  Let no person stint to pay him deference;
  Be not bold to strike, but keep your hearts in patience,
  And to your Lord keep heart of reverence,
  For he, your king, has all puissance!
  In the name of the law, I command you peace!
  And King Herod—"la grandeaboly vos umport."[238]
HEROD. Qui status in Jude et Rex Israel,[239]
  And the mightiest conqueror that ever walked on ground;
  For I am even he that made both heaven and hell,
  And of my mighty power holdeth up this world round.
  Magog and Madroke, both them did I confound,
  And with this bright brand their bones I brake asunder,

---

  [237] to.

  [238] "The devil run away with you!" The whole of this Herald's speech is in corrupt French, of which only the last speech, evidently a comic "aside," is retained.

  [239] He that reigns, King in Judea and Israel.

That all on the wide world on those rappis[240] did wonder.
I am the cause of this great light and thunder;
It is through my fury that they such noise do make.
My fearful countenance the clouds so doth encumber,
That often for dread thereof the very earth doth quake.
Look when I with malin this bright brand doth shake;
All the whole world from the north to the south,
I may them destroy with one word of my mouth,
To recount unto you my innumerable substance
That were too much for any tongue to tell;
For all the whole Orient is under mine obedience,
And prince am I of purgatory, and chief captain of hell.
And those tyrannous traitors by force may I compel
Mine enemies to vanquish, and even to dust to drive,
And with a twinkle of mine eye not one to be left alive.
Behold my countenance and my colour,
Brighter than the sun in the middle of the day!
Where can you have a more greater succour,
Than to behold my person that is so gay;
My falchion and my fashion with my gorgeous array?
He that had the grace always thereon to think,
Live they might alway without other meat or drink.
And this my triumphant fame most highly doth abound,
Throughout this world in all regions abroad,
Resembling the favour of that most mighty Mahound
From Jupiter by descent, and cousin to the great God,
And named the most renowned King Herod,
Which that all princes hath under subjection,
And all their whole power under my protection.
And therefore my herald here called Calchas,
Warn thou every port, that no ships arrive,
Nor also alien stranger through my realm pass,
But they for their truage[241] do pay marks five,
Now speed thee forth hastily,
For they that will the contrary,
Upon a gallows hanged shall be;
And, by Mahound, of me they get no grace.
HERALD. Now, lord and master! in all the haste,
    Thy worthy will it shall be wrought,
    And thy royal countries shall be past,
    In as short time as can be thought.
HEROD. Now shall our regions throughout be sought

---

[240] strokes, loud blows.
[241] tribute.

In every place, both east and west;
If any caitiffs to me be brought,
It shall be nothing for their best.
And the while that I do rest,
Trumpets, viols, and other harmony,
Shall bless the waking of my majesty.

[*Here* HEROD *goeth away, and the three* KINGS *speaketh in the street.*]

1ST KING. Now blessed be God, of his sweet sonde[242]
    For yonder a bright star I do see!
Now is he come us among
As the prophets said that it should be.
    He said there should a babe be born
Coming of the root of Jesse,
To save mankind that was forlorn,
And truly come now is he.
    Reverence and worship to him will I do
As God and man, that all made of nought.
All the prophets accorded and said even so,
That with his precious blood mankind should be bought.
    He grant me grace by yonder star that I see,
And into that place bring me,
That I may him worship with humility
And see his glorious face.
2ND KING. Out of my way I deem that I am
    For tokens of this country can I none see;
Now God that on earth madest man,
Send me some knowledge where that I be.
    Yonder me thinks a fair bright star I see,
The which betokeneth the birth of a child,
That hither is come to make man free,
He, born of a maid, and she nothing defiled,
    To worship that child is mine intent.
Forth now will I take my way:
I trust some company God hath me sent,
For yonder I see a king labour on the way,
    Toward him now will I ride.
Hark, comely king, I you pray,
Into what coast will ye this tide,
Or whither lies your journey?
1ST KING. To seek a child is mine intent,

---

[242] message.

Of whom the prophets have meant.
The time is come now is he sent,
By yonder star here may you see.
2ND KING. Sir, I pray you with your licence,
To ride with you into his presence;
To him will I offer frankincence
For the head of the whole church shall he be.
3RD KING. I ride wandering in ways wide
Over mountains and dales, I wot not where I am,
Now king of all kings send me such guide,
That I may have knowledge of this country's name.
   Ah, yonder I see a sight be seeming all afar,
The which betokens some news as I trow,
As me thinks a child appearing in a star;
I trust he be come that shall defend us from woe.
   Two kings yonder I see, and to them will I ride,
For to have their company: I trust they will me abide.[243]
Hail, comely kings augent![244]
Good sirs, I pray you whither are ye meant?
1ST KING. To seek a child is our intent,
Which betokens yonder star as ye may see.
2ND KING. To him I purpose this present.
3RD KING. Sirs, I pray you, and that right humbly
With you that I may ride in company;
To Almighty God now pray we,
That his precious person we may see.

[*Here* HEROD *cometh in again, and the messenger saith:*]

HERALD. Hail, Lord! most of might!
Thy commandment is right.
Into thy land is come this night
Three kings, and with them a great company.
HEROD. What make those kings in this country?
HERALD. To seek a king and a child, they say.
HEROD. Of what age should he be?
HERALD. Scant twelve days old fully.
HEROD. And was he so late born?
HERALD. Eh! sir, so they show'd me this same day in the morn.
HEROD. Now, in pain of death, bring them me beforn
And, therefore, herald, hie thee now, in haste,
In all speed that thou were dight,[245]

---

[243] await.
[244] (?) and gentle or noble.

Or that those kings the country be past,—
Look thou bring them all three before my sight.
And in Jerusalem enquire more of that child?
But I warn thee that thy words be mild,
For there take thou heed, and craft thereto
His power to foredo,[246]
That those three kings shall be beguiled.

HERALD. Lord, I am ready at your bidding,
    To serve thee as my lord and king,
    For joy thereof, lo, how I spring,
    With light heart and fresh gambolling,
    Aloft here on this mould.

HEROD. Then speed thee forth hastily,
    And look that thou bear thee evenly
    And also I pray thee heartily,
    That thou do commend me
    Both to young and old.

HERALD. [*returning to the* THREE KINGS.] Hail, sir kings, in your
    degree!
    Herod; king of these countries wide
    Desireth to speak with you all three,
    And for your coming he doth abide.

1ST KING. Sir, at his will we be right bane[247]
    Hie us, brother, unto that lord's place;
    To speak with him we would be fain
    That child that we seek, he grant us of his grace.

HERALD. [*bringing in the* KINGS.] Hail, Lord, without peer!
    These three kings have we brought.

HEROD. Now welcome, sir kings, all in fere;[248]
    But of my bright ble,[249] sirs, abash ye nought.
    Sir kings, as I understand,
    A star hath guided you into my land;
    Wherein great harie[250] ye have found,
    By reason of her beams bright;
    Wherefore I pray you heartily,
    The very truth that you would certify;
    How long it is surely,
    Since of that star you had first sight?

1ST KING. Sir king, the very truth we say.

---

[245] prepared.
[246] undo.
[247] prepared, ready.
[248] All in company.
[249] mien, face.
[250] trouble, or from "haro," help.

And to show you, as it is best,
This same is even the twelfth day
Since it appeared to us to be west.

HEROD. Brother, then is there no more to say,
But with heart and will keep ye your journey,
And come home again this same way,
Of your news that I may know.
You shall triumph in this country,
And with great concord banquet with me
And that child myself then will I see,
And honour him also.

2ND KING. Sir, your commandment we will fulfil,
And humbly obey ourselves theretyll,
He that weldeth all things at will.
The ready way us teach,
Sir king, that we may pass your land in peace.

HEROD. Yes! and walk softly even at your own ease.
Your passport for a hundred days
Here shall you have of clear command;
Our realm to labour[251] any ways
Here shall you have by special grant.

3RD KING. Now farewell, king of high degree,
Humbly of you our leave we take.

HEROD. Then adieu, sir kings, all three,
And while I live be bold of me;
There is nothing in this country,
But for your own ye shall it take.

[*Exeunt the* THREE KINGS.]

Now these three kings are gone on their way,
Unwisely and unwittingly have they all wrought.
When they come again, they shall die that same day,
And thus these vile wretches to death shall be brought;
Such is my liking.
He that against my laws will hold,
Be he king or kaiser, never so bold,
I shall them cast into cares cold,
And to death I shall them bring.

[*There* HEROD *goeth his way, and the* THREE KINGS *come in
    again.*]

---

[251] travel.

1ST KING. Oh, blessed God, much is thy might!
    Where is this star that gave us light?
2ND KING. Now kneel we down here on this presence
    By seeking that Lord of high magnificence;
    That we may see his high excellence,
    If that his sweet will be.
3RD KING. Yonder, brother, I see the star,
    Whereby I know he is not far;
    Therefore, lords, go we now,
    Into this poor place.

[*There the* THREE KINGS *go in to the jeseyne,*[252] MARY *and her child.*]

1ST KING. Hail, Lord, that all this world hath wrought!
    Hail God and man together in fere.[253]
    For thou hast made all thing of nought
    Albeit that thou liest poorly here.
    A cup full of gold here I have thee brought
    In tokening thou art without peer.
2ND KING. Hail be thou, Lord of high magnificence
    In tokening of priesthood, and dignity of office,
    To thee I offer a cup full of incense;
    For it behoveth thee to have such sacrifice.
3RD KING. Hail be thou, Lord long looked for!
    I have brought thee myrrh for mortality;
    In tokening those shalt mankind restore
    To life by thy death upon a tree.
MARY. God have mercy, kings, of your goodness!
    By the guiding of the Godhead hither are ye sent;
    The provision of my sweet son, your ways home redress,
    And ghostly reward you for your present.
1ST KING. Sir kings, after our promise,
    Home by Herod, I must needs go.
2ND KING. Now truly, brother, we can no less,
    But I am so far watched I wot not what to do.
3RD KING. Right so am I, wherefore I you pray
    Let all us rest us awhile upon this ground.
1ST KING. Brother, your saying is right well unto my pay
    The grace of that sweet child save us all sound.
ANGEL. King of Taurus, Sir Jaspar!
    King of Araby, Sir Balthasar!

---

[252] childbed, or lying-in chamber.
[253] company.

Melchior, king of Aginara!
To you now am I sent.
For dread of Herod, go you west home
In those parts when ye come down,
Ye shall be burrid[254] with great renown:
The Holy Ghost this knowledge hath sent.
1ST KING. Awake, sir kings, I you pray,
For the voice of an angel I heard in my dream!
2ND KING. That is full true that ye do say
For he rehearsed our names plain.
3RD KING. He bade that we should go down by west
For dread of Herod's false betray.
1ST KING. So for to do it is the best,
The child that we have sought, guide us the way!

[*Turning to the babe.*]

Now farewell, the fairest of shape so sweet,
And thanked be Jesus of his sond.[255]
That we three together so suddenly should meet
That dwell so wide, and in a strange land;
And here to make our presentation
Unto this king's son cleansed so clean,
And to his mother for our salvation;
Of much mirth now may we mean,
That we so well hath done this oblation.
2ND KING. Now farewell, Sir Jaspar, brother to you,
King of Taurus, the most worth;
Sir Balthasar, also to you I bow
And I thank you both of your good company,
While we together have been.
He that made us to meet on hill,
I thank him now, and ever I will;
For now may we go without ill;
And of our offering be full fain.
3RD KING. Now sith that we must needly go
For dread of Herod, that is so wroth,
Now farewell brother, and brother also;
I take my leave here of you both,
This day on foot.
Now he that made us to meet on plain.
And offered to Mary in her jeseyne,[256]

---

[254] go free.
[255] summons.

He give us grace in heaven again,
Altogether to meet.

[*Exeunt the* THREE KINGS: *Enter the* HERALD *and King* HEROD.]

HERALD. Hail, King most worthiest in wede![257]
    Hail, maintainer of courtesy through all this world wide!
    Hail, the most mightiest that ever bestrode a steed!
    Hail, most manfullest man in armour man to abide!
    Hail in thine honour!
    These three kings that forth were sent
    And should have come again before thee here present,
    Another way, Lord, home they went
    Contrary to thine honour.
HEROD. Another way!—out! out!—out!
    Hath those foul traitors done me this deed?
    I stamp, I stare, I look all about;
    Might them I take I should them burn at a glede.[258]
    I rend, I roar, and now run I wood;[259]
    Ah! that these villain traitors hath marred this my mood!
    They shall be hanged if I come them to.

[*Here* HEROD *rages in the pageant, and in the street also.*]

Eh! and that kerne[260] of Bethlehem, he shall be dead,
    And thus shall I do for his prophecy.
    How say you, sir knights, is not this the best red,[261]
    That all young children for this should be dead
    With sword to be slain?
    Then shall I, Herod, live in lede,[262]
    And all folk me doubt and dread,
    And offer to me both gold, riches, and mede,[263]
    Thereto will they be full fain.
1ST SOLDIER. My Lord, King Herod by name,
    Thy words against my will shall be
    To see so many young children die, is shame;
    Therefore counsel thereto gettest thou none of me.

---

[256] childbed.
[257] raiment.
[258] fire.
[259] mad.
[260] wild countryman.
[261] rede, advice.
[262] fame.
[263] reward.

2ND SOLDIER. Well said, fellow, my troth I plight;
    Sir king! perceive right well you may
    So great a murder to see of young fruit,
    Will make a rising in thine own countrey.
HEROD. A rising!—out! out! out!

[*There* HEROD *rages again, and then saith thus:*]

    Out villain wretches, hereupon you I cry,
    My will utterly, look that it be wrought,
    Or upon a gallows both you shall die,
    By Mahound, most mightiest, that me dear hath bought!
1ST SOLDIER. Now, cruel Herod, sith we shall do this deed,
    Your will needfully in this must be wrought.
    All the children of that age, die they must need,
    Now with all my might they shall be upsought.
2ND SOLDIER. And I will swear here upon your bright sword,
    All the children that I find, slain they shall be;
    That make many a mother to weep, and be full sore afeard,
    In our armour bright, when they us see.
HEROD. Now you have sworn, forth that ye go
    And my will that ye work both by day and night,
    And then will I for fain trip like a doe;
    But when they be dead, I warn you, bring them before my sight.
ANGEL. Mary and Joseph, to you I say,
    Sweet word from the Father I bring you full right;
    Out of Bethlehem into Egypt forth go ye the way
    And with you take the king, full of might,
    For dread of Herod's red.[264]
JOSEPH. Arise up, Mary, hastily and soon!
    Our Lord's will needs must be done,
    Like as the angel bade.
MARY. Meekly, Joseph, mine own spouse,
    Toward that country let us repair,
    In Egypt,—some token of house,—
    God grant us grace safe to come there!

[*Here the women come in with their children, singing them, and*
    MARY *and* JOSEPH *goeth clean away.*]

---

[264] order.

Lully, lulla, thou little tiny child;
By, by, lullay, lullay, thou little tiny child;
By, by, lully, lullay.

O sisters too! how may we do,
For to preserve this day
This poor youngling, for whom we do sing
By, by, lully, lullay.

Herod, the king, in his raging,
Charged he hath this day
His men of might, in his own sight,
All young children to slay.

That woe is me, poor child for thee!
And ever morn and day,
For thy parting neither say nor sing,
By, by, lully, lallay.

1ST WOMAN. I lull my child wondrously sweet,
    And in my arms I do it keep,
    Because that it should not cry.
2ND WOMAN. That Babe that is born, in Bethlehem so meek,
    He save my child and me from villainy!
3RD WOMAN. Be still! be still! my little child!
    That Lord of lords save both thee and me;
    For Herod hath sworn with words wild
    That all young children slain they shall be.
1ST SOLDIER. Say ye whither, ye wives, whither are ye away?
    What bear you in your arms needs must we see;
    If they be men children, die they must this day,
    For at Herod's will all things must be.
2ND SOLDIER. And I in hands once them hent,[265]
    Them for to slay nought will I spare;
    We must fulfil Herod's commandment;
    Else be we as traitors, and cast all in care.
1ST WOMAN. Sir knights! of your courtesy
    This day shame not your chivalry,
    But on my child have pity,
    For my sake in this stead;
    For a simple slaughter it were to sloo[266]

---

[265] take.
[266] slay.

Or to work such a child woe
That can neither speak nor go,
Nor never harm did.

2ND WOMAN. He that slays my child in sight,
If that my strokes on him may light,
Be he squire or knight,
I hold him but lost.
See thou false losyngere[267]
A stroke shalt thou bear me here
And spare you no cost.

3RD WOMAN. Sit he never so high in saddle,
But I shall make his brain addle,
And here with my pot ladle,
With him will I fight.
I shall lay on him as though I wode[268] were,
With this same womanly gear;
There shall no man stir,
Whether that he be king or knight.

[*The innocents are massacred.*]

1ST SOLDIER. Who heard ever such a cry
Of women, that their children have lost
And greatly rebuking chivalry
Throughout this realm in every coast
Which many a man's life is like to cost;
For this great revenge that here is done,
I fear much vengeance thereof will come.

2ND SOLDIER. Eh! brother, such tales may we not tell,
Wherefore to the king let us go,
For he is like to bear the bell,
Which was the cause that we did so;
Yet must they all be brought him to
With wains and waggons full freight.
I trow there will be a careful sight.

[*They come before* HEROD.]

1ST SOLDIER. Lo! Herod, king! here must thou see
How many thousands that we have slain.

2ND SOLDIER. And needs thy will fulfilled must be,
There may no man say there again.[269]

---

[267] deceiver.
[268] mad.

HERALD. Herod, king! I shall thee tell,
    All thy deeds is come to nought.
    This child is gone into Egypt to dwell,
    Lo! Sir, in thine own land what wonders byn[270] wrought.
HEROD. Into Egypt? Alas! for woe,
    Longer in land here I cannot abide.
    Saddle my palfry, for in haste will I go
    After yon traitors now will I ride
    Them for to sloo.[271]
    Now all men hie fast
    Into Egypt in haste:
    All that country will I tast[272]
    Till I may come them to.

---

[269] say against it, deny it.
[270] have been.
[271] slay.
[272] explore.

The Wakefield Miracle-Play of the Crucifixion

[FROM THE TOWNELEY COLLECTION]

CHARACTERS

JESUS
MARY
JOHN
JOSEPH
PILATE
LONGEUS
NICODEMUS
FOUR TORTURERS

THE CRUCIFIXION

PILATE. Peace I bid every wight;
    Stand as still as stone in wall,
    Whiles ye are present in my sight,
    That none of ye clatter nor call;
    For if ye do, your death is dight.
    I warn it you both great and small,
    With this brand burnished so bright,
    Therefore in peace look ye be all.

    What? peace, in the devil's name!
    Harlots and dastards all bedene[273]
    On gallows ye be made full tame.
    Thieves and michers ken[274]
    Will ye not peace when I bid you?
    By Mahoun's blood! if ye me teyn,[275]
    I shall ordain soon for you
    Pains that never e'er was seen,
        And that anon:
    Be ye so bold beggars, I warn you,
    Full boldly shall I beat you,
    To hell the de'il shall draw you,
        Body, back, and bone.

    I am a lord that mickle is of might,

---

[273] at once.
[274] know.
[275] vex.

Prince of all Jewry, Sir Pilate I hight.
Next bring Herod, greatest of all,
Bow to my bidding, both great and small,
   Or else be ye shent;[276]
Therefore keep your tongues, I warn you all
   And unto us take tent.[277]
1ST TORTURER. All peace, all peace, among you all!
   And hearken now what shall befall
      To this false chuffer[278] here.
   That with his false quantyse[279]
   Has made himself as God wise
      Among us many a year.
   He calls himself a prophet,
   And says that he can bales[280] beat[281]
      And make all things amend,
   But e'er long know we shall,
   Whether he can overcome his own bale,[280]
      Or 'scape out of our hand.
      Was not this a wonder thing
   That he durst call himself a king
      And make so great a lie?
   But, by Mahoun! while I may live,
   Those proud words shall I never forgive,
      Till he be hanged on high.
2ND TORTURER. His pride, fie, we set at nought,
   But each man reckon in his thought
      And look that we naught want;
   For I shall seek, if that I may,
   By the order of knighthood, to-day,
      To make his heart pant.
3RD TORTURER. And so shall I, with all my might,
   Abate his pride this very night,
      And reckon him a crede.
   Lo! he lets on he could no ill,
   But he can aye, when he will,
      Do a full foul deed.
4TH TORTURER. Ye fellows, ye, as I, have rest,
   Among us all I rede[282] we cast

---

[276] destroyed.
[277] heed.
[278] boaster.
[279] wisdom.
[280] evil.
[281] vanquish.
[282] advise.

To bring this thief to dede.[283]
Look that we have what we need too
   For to hold strait this shrew.
1ST TORTURER. That was a noble rede;
   Lo, here I have a band,
   If need be, to bind his hand;
     This thong, I trow, will last.
2ND TORTURER. And one to the other side,
   That shall abate his pride,
     If it be but drawn fast.
3RD TORTURER. Lo, here a hammer and nails also
   For to fasten fast our foe
     To this tree full soon.
4TH TORTURER. You are wise, withouten dread,
   That so can help yourself at need
     To thing that should be done.
1ST TORTURER. Now dare I say hardily,
   He shall with all his mawmentry[284]
     No longer us be-tell.
2ND TORTURER. Since Pilate has him to us gi'en
   Have done, quickly, let it be seen,
     How we can with him mell.[285]
3RD TORTURER. Now we are at the Mount of Calvary,
   Have done, fellows, and let now see
     How we can with him play.
4TH TORTURER. Yes, for as proud as he can look,
   He would have turned another crook,
     Had he the rack to-day.
1ST TORTURER. In faith, sir, since ye called you a king,
   You must prove a worthy thing
     That falls into the weir.
   You must joust in tournament,
   But sit you fast, else you'll be shent,[286]
     Else down I shall you bear.
2ND TORTURER. If thou be God's son, as thou tells,
   Thou canst save thyself—how shouldst thou else?
     Else were it marvel great;
   And canst thou not, we will not trow
   What thou has said, but make thee mow
     When thou sitt'st in that seat.
3RD TORTURER. If thou be king, we shall thanks adylle[287]

---

[283] death.
[284] idolatry.
[285] meddle.
[286] destroyed.

For we shall set thee in thy sadylle[288]
For falling be thou bold[289]
I promise thee thou bidest a shaft
If thou sitt'st not well thou hadst better laft[290]
The tales that thou hast told.

4TH TORTURER. Stand near, fellows, and let us see
How we can horse our king so free
By any craft;
Stand thou yonder on yon side,
And we shall see how he can ride.
And how to wield a shaft.

1ST TORTURER. Sir, come ye hither, and have done,
And get upon your palfrey soon
For he is ready bowne:[291]
If ye be bound to him be not wroth,
For be ye secure we were full loth
On any wise that ye fell down.

2ND TORTURER. Knit thou a knot, with all thy strength
For to draw this arm at length
Till it come to the bore.

3RD TORTURER. Thou art mad, man, by this light!
It wants, in each man's sight
Another half span, and more.

4TH TORTURER. Yet draw out this arm, and make it fast,
With this rope, that well will last,
And each man lay hand to.

1ST TORTURER. Yes, and bind thou fast that band,
We shall go to that other hand,
And look what we can do.

2ND TORTURER. Do drive a nail there throughout,
And then there shall nothing doubt,
For it will not breste.[292]

3RD TORTURER. That shall I do, so might I thrive,
For to hammer and to drive
Thereto I am full pressed;
So let it stick, for it is well.

4TH TORTURER. Thou sayest sooth,
There can no man mend.

1ST TORTURER. Hold down his knees.

---

[287] a-deal.
[288] saddle.
[289] i.e. Be not afraid to fall.
[290] left unsaid.
[291] prepared.
[292] burst.

2ND TORTURER. That shall I do.
 His nurse did never better do;
  Lay on with each hand.
3RD TORTURER. Draw out his limbs, let see, have at.
4TH TORTURER. That was well drawn out, that,
 Fair befall him that so pulled!
 For to have gotten it to the mark
 I trow laymen nor clerk
  Nothing better should!
1ST TORTURER. Hold it now fast there
 One of you the bore shall bear,
  And then it may not fail.
2ND TORTURER. That shall I do withouten dread,
 As ever might I well speed
  Him to mickle bale.
3RD TORTURER. So, that is well, it will not brest,[293]
 But now, let see, who does the best
  With any sleight of hand.
4TH TORTURER. Go we to the other ende
 Fellows, fasten fast your hende,[294]
  And pull well at the band.
1ST TORTURER. I counsel, fellows, by this weather
 That we draw now all together,
  And look how it will fare.
2ND TORTURER. Now let see, and leave your din
 And draw we ilka syn from syn.[295]
  For nothing let us spare.
3RD TORTURER. Nay, fellows, this is no play,
 We no longer draw one way,
  So mickle have I espied.
4TH TORTURER. No, for as I have bliss
 Some can twig whoso it is
  Seeks his ease on his own side.
1ST TORTURER. It is better, as I hope
 Each by himself to draw this rope,
 And then may we see
 Who it is that erewhile
 All his fellows can beguile
  Of this company.
2ND TORTURER. Since thou wilt so have, here's for me!
 How draw I?—as might thou the![296]

---

[293] burst.
[294] hands.
[295] each sinew from sinew.
[296] so may you thrive.

3RD TORTURER. Men drew right well!
　Have here for me, half a foot.
4TH TORTURER. Wema,[297] man! thou came not to't.
　Men drew it never a deal
　But have for me here that I may!
1ST TORTURER. Well drawnën, son, by this day!
　Thou goes well to thy work.
2ND TORTURER. Yet after, whilst thy hand is in
　　Pull thereat with some engine.
3RD TORTURER. Yea, and bring it to the mark.
4TH TORTURER. Pull, pull!
1ST TORTURER. Have now!
2ND TORTURER. Let see!
3RD TORTURER. Aha!
4TH TORTURER. Yet, a draught!
1ST TORTURER. Thereto with all my might.
2ND TORTURER. Aha, hold still thore.[298]
3RD TORTURER. So, fellows, look now alive,
　　Which of you can best drive,
　　　And I shall take the bore.
4TH TORTURER. Let me go to it, if I shall
　　I hope that I be the best marshal[299]
　　　For to clink[300] it right.
　Do raise him up now when we may,
　For I hope he and his palfrey
　　Shall not twine[301] this night.
1ST TORTURER. Come hither, fellows, and have done,
　　And help that this tree soon
　　　Be lift with all your sleight.
2ND TORTURER. Yet let us work awhile,
　　And no man now the other beguile
　　　Till it be brought on height.
3RD TORTURER. Fellows, lay on all your hende[302]
　　For to raise this tree on ende
　　　And lets see who is last.
4TH TORTURER. I rede we do as he says,
　　Set we the tree on the mortase,[303]
　　　And there, will it stand fast.

---

[297] Good Lord!
[298] there.
[299] smith.
[300] hammer.
[301] part.
[302] hands.
[303] mortice (the hole cut in the ground-piece).

1ST TORTURER. Up with the timber.
2ND TORTURER. Ah, it holds!
    For him, that all this world wields,
      Put from thee, with thy hand.
3RD TORTURER. Hold even! amongst us all.
4TH TORTURER. Yea, and let it into the mortise fall,
    For then will it best stand.
1ST TORTURER. Go we to it, and be we strong,
    And raise it, be it never so long,
      Since that it is fast bound.
2ND TORTURER. Up with the timber fast on ende.
3RD TORTURER. Ah fellows, fair fall now your hende.
4TH TORTURER. So, sir, gape against the sun!
1ST TORTURER. [*To* CHRIST.] Ah, fellow, wear thy crown!
2ND TORTURER. Trowest thou this timber will come down?
3RD TORTURER. Yet help, to make it fast.
4TH TORTURER. Bind him well, and let us lift.
1ST TORTURER. Full short shall be his thrift.
2ND TORTURER. Ah, it stands up like a mast.
JESUS. I pray you, people, that pass me by,
    That lead your life so lykandly[304]
      Raise up your heart on high;
    Behold if ever ye saw body
    Buffet[305] and beaten thus bloody,
      Or dight thus dolefully;
    In this world was never no wight
      That suffered half so sair.
    My mayn,[306] my mode,[307] my might
    Is naught but sorrow to sight,
      And comfort—none but care!
    My folk, what have I done to thee
    That thou all thus shall torment me?
      Thy sin bear I full soon.
    How have I grieved thee? answer me.
    That thou thus nailest me to a tree,
      And all for thine error.
    Where shalt thou seek succour?
    This fault how shalt thou amende
    When that thou thy saviour
    Drivest to this dishonour
      And nail'st through feet and hende.[308]

---

[304] pleasantly.
[305] buffeted.
[306] strength.
[307] mood.

All creatures whose kinds may be trest,[309]
Beasts and birds, they all have rest
   When they are woe begone.
But God's own son, that should be best,
Has not whereon his head to rest,
   But on his shoulder bone:
To whom now may I make my moan
   When they thus martyr me?
And sackless[310] will me slone,[311]
And beat me blood and bone,
   That should my brethren be?
What kindness should I kythe[312] them to?
Have I not done what I ought to do,
   Made thee in my likeness?
And thou thus rives my rest and ro[313]
And thinkest lightly on me, lo,
   Such is thy caitifness.
I have shown thee kindness, unkindly thou me 'quitest,[314]
See thus thy wickedness, look how thou me despitest.
Guiltless thus am I put to pine,
Not for my sin, man, but for thine.
   Thus am I rent on rood;
For I that treasure would not tyne[315]
That I marked and made for mine.
   Thus buy I Adam's blood,
That sunken was in sin,
With none earthly good,
But with my flesh and blood
That loath was for to wyn.[316]
My brother, that I came for to buy,
Has hanged me here, thus hideously,
   Friends find I few or none;
Thus have they dight me drearily,
And all be-spit me piteously,
   A helpless man in wone.[317]
But, Father, that sittest on throne,

---

[308] hands.
[309] cast up.
[310] guiltless.
[311] slay.
[312] shew.
[313] repose.
[314] requitest.
[315] lose.
[316] labour.
[317] in wont.

Forgive thou them this guilt.
I pray to thee this boon—
They know not what they doon,
  Nor whom they thus have spoilt![318]
1ST TORTURER. Yes, what we do full well we know.
2ND TORTURER. Yes, that shall he find within a throw.
3RD TORTURER. Now, with a mischance to his corse!
  Wenys[319] he that we give any force[320]
    What evil so ever he ail?
4TH TORTURER. For he would tarry us all day,
  Of his death to make delay,
    I tell you sans fail.
1ST TORTURER. Lift we this tree amongst us all.
2ND TORTURER. Yea, and let it into the mortise fall
  And that shall make him brest.[321]
3RD TORTURER. Yea, and all to rive him, limb from limb.
4TH TORTURER. And it will break each joint in him;
  Let see now, who does best?
MARY. Alas, the dole I dree![322] I droop, I go in dread.
  Why hang'st thou, son, so high? my woe begins to breed,
  All blemished is thy ble,[323] I see thy body bleed,
  In the world, my son, we were never so woe, as now in weed.[324]
  My food[325] that I have fed,
  In life—longing thee led!
  Full straight art thou bestead
    Among these foemen fell:
  Such sorrow for to see.
  My dearest child, on thee,
  Is more mourning to me
    Than any tongue may tell.
  Alas! thy holy head
  Has not whereon to held[326]
  Thy face with blood is red,
  Was fair as flower in field
  How should I stand in stead![327]
  To see my bairn thus bleed,

---

[318] despoiled, destroyed.

[319] thinks, knows.

[320] i.e. Does he think we care how he suffers?

[321] burst.

[322] the grief I bear.

[323] face, visage.

[324] garments, aspect.

[325] nurseling, fed child.

[326] hold, rest.

[327] how should I stand still in my place.

Beaten as blo[328] as lead.
    And has no limb to wield?
Fastened both hands and feet,
With nalys[329] full unmeet,
His wounds all wringing wet.
    Alas, my child, for care!
For all rent is thy hide,
I see on either side
Tears of blood down glide
    Over all thy body bare.
Alas that ever I should bide, and see my feyr[330] thus fare!

JOHN. Alas, for dule, my lady dear!
    All for changèd is thy cheer,
    To see this prince without a peer,
        Thus lappéd all in woe;
    He was thy food, thy fairest foine,[331]
    Thy love, thy like,[332] thy lovesome son,
    That high on tree thus hangs alone
        With body black and blo,[333] alas!
    To me and many mo,[334]
    A good master he was.
    But, lady, since it is his will
    The prophecy to fulfil,
    That mankind in sin not spill,[335]
        For them to thole[336] the pain;
    And with his death ransom to make,
    As prophets before of him spake.
    I counsel thee, thy grief to slake,
        Thy weeping may not gain
    In sorrow;
    Our boot[337] he buys full bayne,[338]
    Us all from bale to borrow.

MARY. Alas, thine eyes as crystal clear,
    That shone as sun in sight,
    That lovely were in lyere[339]

---

[328] blue.
[329] nails.
[330] companion.
[331] treasure.
[332] liking.
[333] blue.
[334] more.
[335] perish.
[336] bear.
[337] good, gain.
[338] hard, dearly.

Lost they have their light,
And wax all fa'ed[340] in fear,
All dim then are they dight;
In pain thou hast no peer,
That is withouten pight.[341]
Sweet son, say me thy thought;
What wonders hast thou wrought
To be in pain thus brought
 Thy blessed blood to blend?
Ah, son, think on my woe,
Why will thou from me go?
On earth is no man mo[342]
 That may my mirth amend.

JOHN. Comely lady, good and couth,[343]
 Fain would I comfort thee;
Me mynnys[344] my master with mouth
Told unto his menyee.[345]
That he should suffer many a pain,
And die upon a tree,
And to the life rise up again,
Upon the third day should it be
 Full right;
For thee, my lady sweet,
Stint awhile to greet,[346]
Our bale then will be beat,[347]
 As he before has bight.[348]

MARY. My sorrow it is so sad,
 No solace may me save:
Mourning makes me mad,
No hope of help I have.
I am redeless[349] and afraid
For fear that I should rave,
Nought may make me glad,
Till I be in my grave.
To death my dear is driven,

---

[339] flesh.
[340] faded.
[341] doubt.
[342] more.
[343] fair, the opposite of uncouth.
[344] Methinks.
[345] followers.
[346] weep.
[347] He will beat down our fall or evil, as he promised.
[348] promised.
[349] without counsel.

His robe is all to-riven,[350]
That by me was him given
  And shapen with my sides.
These Jews and he have striven
  That all the bale he bides.
Alas! my lamb so mild,
Why wilt thou from me go
Among these wolvés wild,
That work on thee this woe?
For shame, who may thee shield,
For friends now hast thou foe.
Alas, my comely child,
Why will thou from me go?
Maidens, make your moan,
And weep, ye wives, every one
With me, most sad, in wone[351]
  The child that born was best:
My heart is stiff as stone
  That for no bale will brest.[352]

JOHN. Ah, lady, well wot I,
  Thy heart is full of care,
  When thou thus openly
  Seest thy child thus fare;
  Love drives him rathly.
  Himself he will not spare,
  Us all from bale to buy,
  Of bliss that are full bare
  For sin;
  My dear lady, therefore of mourning look thou blyn.[353]

MARY. "Alas!" may ever be my song,
  While I may live in leyd,[354]
  Methinks now that I live too long,
  To see my bairn thus bleed.
  Jews work with him all wrong,
  Wherefore do they this deed?
  Lo, so high have they him hung,
  They let[355] for no dread;
    Why so?
  His foeman he is among.

---

[350] torn.
[351] in wont, habitually.
[352] burst for no grief.
[353] cease.
[354] grief.
[355] stay.

No friend he has, but foe,
My frely food[356] from me must go
What shall become of me?
Thou art warpyd[357] all in woe,
  And spread here on a tree
    Full hie;[358]
I mourn, and so may mo[359]
That see this pain on thee.

JOHN. Dear lady, well for me
  If that I might comfort thee,
  For the sorrow that I see
    Shears my heart in sunder;
  When that I see my master hang
  With bitter pains and strong;
  Was never wight with[360] wrong
    Wrought so mickle wonder.

MARY. Alas, death, thou dwellest too long,
  Why art thou hid from me?
  Who bid thee to my child to gang?[361]
  All black thou mak'st his ble;[362]
  Now witterly,[363] thou workest wrong
  The more I will wyte[364] thee.
  But if thou wilt my heart now sting
  That I may with him dee,[365]
    And bide.
  Sore sighing is my song. For pierced is his side!
    Ah, death, what hast thou done?
  With thee will I fare soon,
  Since I had children none but one,
  Best under sun or moon.
  Friends I had full foyn[366]
  That gars me greet[367] and groan
    Full sore.
  Good Lord, grant me my boon,

---

[356] noble babe.
[357] clothed.
[358] high.
[359] more.
[360] against wrong.
[361] go.
[362] face, complexion.
[363] surely.
[364] blame.
[365] die.
[366] few.
[367] weep.

And let me live no more!
Gabriel! that art so good
Sometime thou did me greet,
And then I understood
Thy words that were so sweet.
But now they vex my mood,
For grace thou canst me hete,[368]
To bear all of my blood
A child our bale should beat[369]
    With right.
Now hangs he here on rood,
Where is that thou me hight.[370]
All that thou of bliss
Hight me in that stede[371]
From mirth is far amiss.
And yet I trow thy rede[372]
Counsel me now of this,
My life how shall I lead
When from me gone is
He that was my head
    On high?
My death, now, come it is:
My dear son, have mercy!

JESUS. My mother mild, change thou thy cheer,
    Cease from thy sorrow and sighing sere,
      It syttes[373] unto my heart full sore;
    The sorrow is sharp, I suffer here;
    But the dole thou drees,[374] my mother dear,
    Me martyrs mickle more.
    Thus wills my father I fare
      To loose mankind from bands
    His son will he not spare,
    To loose that bond was e'er
      Full fast in fiends' hands.
    The first cause, mother, of my coming
    Was for mankind miscarrying,
      To save them sore I sought;
    Therefore, mother make no mourning

---

[368] promised.
[369] beat down our bale, or evil.
[370] promised.
[371] place.
[372] believe thy word.
[373] pricks.
[374] dole, or grief thou endurest.

Since mankind, through my dying,
  May thus to bliss be brought.
Woman, weep thou right nought,
  Take there, John, unto thy child,
Mankind must needs be bought;
And thou cast, cousin, in thy thought.[375]
  John, lo, there, thy mother mild!
Blue and bloody thus am I beat,
Swongen with swepys[376] and all a-sweat,
  Mankind, for thy misdeed.
For my love's sake when wouldst thou let,[377]
And thy heart sadly set,
  Since I thus for thee have bled?
Such life for sooth, I lead,
That nothing may I more.
This I suffer for thy need,
To mark thee, man, thy meed!
  Now thirst I wonder sore.

1ST TORTURER. Nought but hold thy peace,
  Thou shalt have drink within a resse,[378]
    Myself shall be thy knave;
Have here the draught that I thee hete,[379]
  And I shall warrant it is not sweet
    By all the good I have.

2ND TORTURER. So, sir, say now all your will,
  For if ye could have holden you still
    Ye had not had this brade.[380]

3RD TORTURER. Thou would'st all gate[381] be King of Jews,
  But by this I trow thou rues
    All that thou has said.

4TH TORTURER. He has him rused of great prophës[382]
  That he should make us tempyllës
    And make it clean fall down;
And yet he said he should it raise
As well as it was within three days,
  He lies, that wot we all;
And for his lies in great despite

---

[375] cast about, cousin, in thy thought.

[376] swinged with whips.

[377] cease.

[378] reed.

[379] offer.

[380] trouble.

[381] at all costs.

[382] pretended great prophecies.

We will divide his clothing tyte[383]
    Save he can more of art.[384]
1ST TORTURER. Yes, as ever might I thrive,
    Soon will we this mantle rive,
      And each man take his part.
2ND TORTURER. How, wouldst thou we share this cloth?
3RD TORTURER. Nay, forsooth, that were I loth,
    For then it were all gate[385] spoilt.
    But assent thou to my saw,[386]
    And let us all cut draw[387]
    And then is none begylt.[388]
2ND TORTURER. Howe'er befall, now I draw,
    This is mine by common law,
      Say not there again.
1ST TORTURER. Now since it may no better be,
    Chevithe thee with it for me;
      Methinks thou art full fain.
2ND TORTURER. How, fellows, see ye not yon scraw?[389]
    It is written yonder within a thraw,
      Now since that we drew lot.
3RD TORTURER. There is no man that is alive,
    Unless Pilate, as I might thrive
      That durst it there have put.
4TH TORTURER. Go we fast, and let us look
    What is written on yon book
      And what it may be, mean.
1ST TORTURER. All the more I look thereon,
    All the more I think I fon;[390]
      All is not worth a bean.
2ND TORTURER. Yes for sooth, methinks I see
    Thereon written language three
      Hebrew and Latýn
    And Greek methinks written thereon,
    For it is hard for to expoun.
3RD TORTURER. Thou read, by Apollyon!
4TH TORTURER. Yea, as I am a true knight.
    I am the best Latin wright

---

[383] quickly.
[384] unless he can shew still further craft, or art.
[385] all ways, quite.
[386] Saying, as in a wise saw.
[387] draw lots.
[388] beguiled.
[389] scroll.
[390] am bewildered.

      Of this company;
I will go withouten delay
And tell you what it is to say.
      Behold, sirs, verily,
Yonder is written—Jesus of Nazarene
He is King of Jews, I ween.

1ST TORTURER. Ah, that is written wrong.

2ND TORTURER. He calls himself so, but he is none.

3RD TORTURER. Go we to Pilate and make our moan,
      Have done, and dwell not long. [*They go to* PILATE.]
      Pilate, yonder is a false table,
      Thereon is written naught but fable,
        Of Jews he is not king,
      He calls him so, but he not is,
      It is falsely written, I wis,
        This is a wrong-wise thing.

PILATE. Boys, I say, what melle ye yon?[391]
      As it is written shall it be now,
        I say certain
      Quod scriptum scripsi,[392]
      That same wrote I,
        What gadlyng[393] grumbles there again.

4TH TORTURER. Since that he is a man of law
      He must needs have his will;
      I trow he had not written that saw
      Without some proper skill.

1ST TORTURER. Yea, let it hang above his head
      It shall not save him from the dead
        Naught that he can write.

2ND TORTURER. Now ill a hale[394] was he born!

3RD TORTURER. My faith, I tell his life is lorn
        He shall be slain as tyte.[395]
      If thou be Christ, as men thee call
      Come down now among us all
        And thole[396] not these missays.[397]

4TH TORTURER. Yea, and help myself that we may see
      And we shall all believe in thee,
        Whatsoever thou says.

---

[391] What meddle ye with?

[392] What I wrote is written.

[393] fellow.

[394] ill fall the day.

[395] quickly.

[396] bear.

[397] insults, miscallings.

1ST TORTURER. He calls himself good of might,
But I would see him be so wight[398]
To do such a deed.
He raised Lazare out of his delf[399]
But he cannot help himself
Now in his great need.

JESUS. Eli, Eli, lama sabacthani!
My God, my God! wherefor and why
Hast thou forsaken me?

2ND TORTURER. How, hear ye not as well as I
How he can upon Eli cry
Upon this wise?

3RD TORTURER. Yea, there is no Eli in this country
Shall deliver him from this meneye[400]
No, in no wise.

4TH TORTURER. I warrant you now at the last
That he shall soon yield the ghost
For bursten is his gall.

JESUS. Now is my passion brought to end,
Father of heaven, into thy hende[401]
I do commend my soul.

1ST TORTURER. Let one prick him with a spear,
And if it should do him no dere[402]
Then is his life near past.

2ND TORTURER. This blind knight may best do that.

LONGEUS. Gar me not do, save I wit what.

3RD TORTURER. Naught, but strike up fast.

LONGEUS. Ah! Lord, what may this be?
Once I was blind, now I can see;
Gode's son, hear me, Jesu!
For this trespass on me thou rue[403]
For, Lord, other men me gart[404]
That I thee struck unto the heart,
I see thou hangest here on high,
And dies to fulfil the prophecy.

4TH TORTURER. Go we hence, and leave him here
For I shall be his bail, this year
He feels now no more pain;

---

[398] knowing, willing.
[399] grave.
[400] host of men, company.
[401] hands.
[402] harm.
[403] have compassion.
[404] compelled.

For Eli, ne for none other man
All the good that ever he won
 Gets not his life again.

[*Exeunt* TORTURERS.]

JOSEPH. Alas, alas, and well a way!
 That ever I should abide this day
  To see my master dead;
 Thus wickedly as he is shent,
 With so bitter tornament[405]
  Thro' the false Jews' red.[406]
 Nicodeme, I would we yede[407]
 To Sir Pilate, if we might spede
  His body for to crave;
 I will strive with all my might
 For my service to ask that knight,
  His body for to grave.[408]
NICODEMUS. Joseph, I will wend with thee
 For to do what is in me
  For that body to pray;
 For our good-will and our travail
 I hope that it may us avail
  Hereafterward some day.
JOSEPH. Sir Pilate, God thee save!
 Grant me what I crave
  If that it be thy will.
PILATE. Welcome, Joseph, might thou be,
 What so thou askest, I grant it thee
  So that it be skill.[409]
JOSEPH. For my long service, I thee pray,
 Grant me the body, say me not nay
  Of Jesus dead on rood.
PILATE. I grant it well if he dead be,
 Good leave shalt thou have of me.
  Do with him what thou think good.
JOSEPH. Gramercy, sir, of your good grace
 That you did grant me in this place.
  Go we our way:
 Nicodeme, come me forth with,

---

[405] torment.
[406] counsel.
[407] were gone.
[408] put in grave.
[409] in reason.

    For I myself shall be the smith
    The nails out for to dray.[410]
NICODEMUS. Joseph, I am ready here
    To go with thee with full good cheer
      To help with all my might.
    Pull forth the nails on either side
    And I shall hold him up this tide;
      Ah, Lord, how art thou dight!

[They take down the body.]

JOSEPH. Help now, fellow, with all thy might,
    That he be wounden[411] and well dight,
      And lay him on this bier:
    Bear we him forth into the kirk
    To the tomb that I gar'd[412] work
      Since full many a year.
NICODEMUS. It shall be so, withouten nay,
    He that died on Good Friday,
      And crownèd was with thorn;
    Save you all that now here be
    That Lord that thus would dee,
      And rose on Paschë[413] morn.

---

[410] draw.
[411] wound in his shroud.
[412] caused them to make.
[413] Easter.

The Cornish Mystery-Play of the Three Maries

CHARACTERS

THE GARDENER—JESUS CHRIST
THE THREE MARIES—
    MARY MAGDALENE
    MARY, MOTHER OF JAMES
    MARY SALOME
FIRST ANGEL
SECOND ANGEL

THE MYSTERY OF THE THREE MARIES

[*Enter* MARY MAGDALENE, *and* MARY, *mother of* JAMES.]

MARY MAGDALENE. What shall I do, alas!
    My Lord went to the tomb,
      To-day is the third day;
    Go now see indeed
    If he comes and rises,
      As he said to me truly.
MARY, MOTHER OF JAMES. I will go and see
    The body of him who redeemed me with pain,
      If it be risen again.
    Great comfort he was to us;
    That we should have seen his death!
      Alas! alas!

[*Enter* MARY SALOME.]

MARY SALOME. The third day is to-day;
    If the body of Christ be risen,
      Go to see.
    For the torment which he had
    Is ever in my heart;
      This sorrow does not leave me.

[*Here she shall meet the other* MARIES.]

MARY MAGDALENE. Women, joy to ye!
    And Mary, mother of James,
      And Salome also.
    Sorrow is in my heart, alas!

If the body of God himself is gone,
  Where may it be found?
MARY, MOTHER OF JAMES. So it is with me,
  Much and great torment for him;
    If he will not, through his grace,
  Help me in a short time,
  My heart in me will break
    Very really through troubles.
MARY SALOME. So with me is sorrow
  May the Lord see my state
    After him.
  As he is head of sovereignty,
  I believe that out of the tomb
    To-day he will rise.
MARY MAGDALENE. Oh! let us hasten at once,
  For the stone is raised
  From the tomb.
  Lord, how will it be this night,
  If I know not where goes
  The head of royalty?
MARY, MOTHER OF JAMES. And too long we have stayed,
  My Lord is gone his way
    Out of the tomb, surely.
  Alas! my heart is sick;
  I know not indeed if I shall see him,
    Who is very God.
MARY SALOME. I know truly, and I believe it,
  That he is risen up
    In this day.
  How will it be to us now,
  That we find not our Lord?
    Alas! woe! woe!

[*They sing.*]

[*The Dirge.*]

Alas! mourning I sing, mourning I call,
Our Lord is dead that bought us all.

MARY MAGDALENE. Alas! it is through sorrows,
  My sweet Lord is dead
    Who was crucified.

[MARY MAGDALENE *weeps at the tomb.*]

He bore, without complaining,
Much pain on his dear body,
   For the people of the world
MARY, MOTHER OF JAMES. I cannot see the form
Of him on any side;
   Alas! woe is me!
I would like to speak with him,
If it were his will,
   Very seriously.
MARY SALOME. There is to me sharp longing
In my heart always,
   And sorrow;
Alas! my Lord Jesus,
For thou art full of virtue,
   All mighty.

[*The Dirge.*]

Alas! mourning I sing, mourning I call,
Our Lord is dead that bought us all.

MARY MAGDALENE. Jesus Christ, Lord of Heaven,
O hear now our voice;
Who believes not in thee, miserable he!
   He will not be saved.
When I think of his Passion,
There is not any joy in my heart;
Alas! that I cannot at once
   Speak to thee.
MARY, MOTHER OF JAMES. Gone he is to another land,
And with him many angels;
Alas! now for grief
   I am sorrowful.
I pray thee, Lord of grace,
To send a messenger to us,
That something we may be knowing
   How it is to thee.
MARY SALOME. O Jesus, full of mercy,
Do think of us;
To thy kingdom when we come,
   Hear our voice.
For desire I become very sick,
I cannot stand on my standing,
Alas! now what shall I do?
   O Lord of heaven!

[*The Dirge.*]

Alas! mourning I sing, mourning I call,
Our Lord is dead, that bought us all.

1ST ANGEL. I know whom ye seek:
    Jesus is not here,
      For he is risen
    To life in very earnest,
    As I tell you,
      Like as he is worthy.

MARY MAGDALENE. O angel, now tell me,
    The body (none, equal to him),
      To what place is it gone?
    Like as his grace is great,
    Joy to me, with my eyes
      To see him yet.

2ND ANGEL. O Mary, go forthwith,
    Say to his disciples
      And to Peter,
    Like as he promised to them
    He will go to Galilee,
      Very truly without doubt.

MARY, MOTHER OF JAMES. Now he is risen again indeed,
    Jesus our Saviour,
      Gone from the tomb.
    Worship to him always;
    He is Lord of heaven and earth,
      Head of sovereignty.

MARY SALOME. Hence go we to the city,
    And let us say in every place
      As we have seen:
    That Jesus is risen,
    And from the tomb forth gone,
      To heaven really.

MARY MAGDALENE. Never to the city shall I go,
    If I do find not my Lord,
      Who was on the cross tree.
    O Jesus, King of grace,
    Joy to me once to see thee,
      Amen, amen.

MARY, MOTHER OF JAMES. Mary, be with thee
    All the blessings of women,
      And the blessing of Jesus Son of grace;
    Of full heart I pray him,
    Joy and grace always good to do

To us now, from God the Father.

MARY MAGDALENE. My blessing on ye also,
 From Christ, as he is gone to the tomb,
  Joy to ye to do well to-day.
 Lord, give me the grace
 Once to see thy face,
  If it be thy will with thee.

MARY SALOME. Amen, amen, let us seek
 Christ, who redeemed us in pain,
  With his flesh and with his blood;
 Much pain he suffered,
 For love of the people of the world,
  As he is the King of power.

[*Here* MARY, *the mother of* JAMES, *and* SALOME *retire from the tomb, and sit down a little way from it.*]

MARY MAGDALENE. He who made heaven, · as he is gone to the tomb,
 After him · great is my desire.
 Christ, hear my voice, · I pray also
 That thou be with me · at my end.

 Lord Jesus, · give me the grace,
 As I may be worthy · to find a meeting,
 With thee to-day, · in some sure place,
 That I may have a view · and sight of thy face.

 As thou art Creator · of heaven and earth,
 And a Redeemer · to us always,
 Christ my Saviour, · hear, if it regards thee
 Disclose to me, · what I so much desire.

 Through great longing · I am quite weary,
 And my body also, · bones and back.
 Where is there to-night · any man who knows
 Where I may yet find · Christ full of sorrow.

[*She goes to the garden.*]

[*Enter the* GARDENER.]

GARDENER (JESUS). O woeful woman, · where goest thou?
 For grief thou prayest, · cry out thou dost.
 Weep not nor shriek, · he whom thou seekest
 Thou didst dry his feet · with thy two plaits.

MARY MAGDALENE. Good lord, · if thou hast chanced to see

Christ my Saviour, · where is he truly?
To see him · I give thee my land;
Jesus, Son of grace, · hear my desire.
GARDENER. O Mary, · as I know thee to be
Within this world, · one of his blood,
If thou shouldst see him · before thee,
Couldst thou · know him?
MARY MAGDALENE. Well I do, · know the form
Of the son of Mary, · named Jesus;
Since I see him not · in any place,
I feel sorrow; · else I would not sing "alas!"

[*And then* JESUS *shall shew his side to* MARY MAGDALENE, *and
say:*]

GARDENER. Mary, see · my five wounds,
Believe me truly · to be risen;
To thee I give thanks · for thy desire,
Joy in the land · there shall be truly.
MARY MAGDALENE. O dear Lord, · who wast on the cross tree,
To me it becomes not · to kiss thy head.
I would pray thee · let me dare
Now to kiss · once thy feet.

[*Woman, touch me not!*]

GARDENER. O woeful woman, · touch me not near,
No, it will not serve, · nor be for gain;
    The time is not come;
Until I go · to heaven to my Father,
And I will return · again to my country,—
    To speak with thee.
MARY MAGDALENE. Christ, hear my voice, · say the hour
That thou comest from heaven · again to earth
    To speak with us.
Thy disciples · are very sad,
And the Jews · with violence always
    Are round about them.
GARDENER. O Mary, · tell them,
Truly I go · to Galilee,
    As I said;
And besides that, · bear in memory to speak
Good comfort · to Peter by me;
    Much he is loved.

The Cornish Mystery-Play of Mary Magdalene

AND HOW SHE BROUGHT THE NEWS OF THE RESURRECTION
OF OUR LORD JESUS CHRIST TO THE APOSTLES

CHARACTERS

JESUS
MARY MAGDALENE
THOMAS
PETER
ANDREW
JOHN
JAMES THE GREATER
JAMES THE LESS
MATTHEW
PHILIP
SIMON
JUDAH

THE MYSTERY OF MARY MAGDALENE AND THE APOSTLES

[*Now* MARY *comes to the apostles, and says to them in Galilee:*]

MARY MAGDALENE. Now, O apostles,
 I will tell you news:
Jesus is risen from the tomb;
 I saw him lately,
I spoke to him also,
 I looked on his wounds,
Pitiful it was to see them;
 To the world they bring healing.
THOMAS. Silence, woman, with thy tales,
 And speak truth, as I pray thee;
Christ who was cruelly slain,
 To be alive I will not believe;
Waste no more words,
 For lies I do not love;
Our Lord is dead;
 Alas! I tell the truth.
MARY MAGDALENE. I speak true, Thomas,
 And I, though poor, will prove it.
Lately I saw him,—
 The Lord (none equal to him),

And by me he sent,
  I swear to ye, as ye may know,
    Like as he promised;
    He named to me none but Peter.

THOMAS. Silence, and speak not, woman!
  I pray thee, mockery with us
    Now do not make;
    Stout though Castle Maudlen be,
    If thou mock, I will break thy head
    About thee from above.

MARY MAGDALENE. I will not be silent from fear
  I will prove it true what I say
    Before we separate.
    Like as he is King of heaven,
    He is with God the Father,
    On his right side.

PETER. Ah! Jesus Christ, happy am I
  To hear that he is risen
    Out of the tomb;
    For I know very well
    That he is son to Mary,
    And God likewise.

THOMAS. Peter, peace, and leave thy mockery,
  For idle it is to say
    That he is risen.
    Never can, for the world,
    Any man be raised
    After dying.

JAMES THE GREATER. Thomas, very well it may be;
  The Son of God will rise
    When he will;
    For Jesus, Son of Mary,
    He made heaven, and this world,
    And every thing that was not.

THOMAS. O James, it is no use for thee;
  A man who is dead certainly
    Does not live again.
    Foolish idleness, not to leave it,
    But to go to assert
    A thing of no benefit.

JOHN. O Thomas, thou art a fool;
  That is the belief of all:
    Jesus Christ after dying,
    To be put into the ground;
    After that to rise again

At the end of three days, and to stand up.

THOMAS. O John, be not absurd,
    For my wonder,—it is great,
      That thou shouldst speak folly.
    Christ through sufferings was
    Indeed put to death on the cross tree;
      My curse on him that did it!

BARTHOLOMEW. Thomas, believe me, though I am gray;
    Man could not have power
      To put him to death.
    For us he would die,
    And go into the tomb, and rise,
      To carry all Christians to heaven.

THOMAS. O Bartte, thou art mad
    And fond beyond all men
      Who are fools.
    God, without dying, might have
    Caused all men to be saved,
      Over all the world.

MATTHEW. That is true, he could
    Destroy every thing again,
      That it be no more.
    But nevertheless for us,
    Christ wished to go into the ground,
      And to live again.

THOMAS. And thou art a fool, Matthew;
    If thou art wise thou wilt be silent,
      And withdraw.
    He lives not, through all thy words,
    When I saw him, he was dead
      On the cross tree.

PHILIP. Alas! to be so foolish!
    Crooked, wilt thou not believe
      The Head of sovereignty;
    And he saying to us
    That after dying he would rise
      Out of the tomb?

THOMAS. Sit silent, wilt thou, Philip,
    For in faith thou swearest wrongly
      About him.
    Christ's limbs were bruised,
    And on his body a thousand wounds;
      Alas! he is not risen.

JAMES THE GREATER. O do not say so,
    That Jesus the best Lord

Cannot rise,
For very truly he is risen;
To be his servant thou art not worthy,
    It appears well.
THOMAS. O thou James, if he were alive
    His servant I would be
        Very joyfully.
    But he is not alive, leave off thy noise;
    The thorn even into his brain,
        Went to his head.
SIMON. Though the thorn went into his head,
    And through his heart and side
        The spear was seen,
    Nevertheless need is to believe
    Jesus Christ will rise again,
        As he is true God.
THOMAS. O Simon, do not speak a word;
    Never, never, unhappily,
        He has not risen again.
    But if it were so,
    Together we should all be
        Exceedingly at ease.
JUDAH. Sir Thomas, it is so,
    He has risen again to-day
        Out of the tomb.
    For if he should not rise again,
    Never with us would there be
        Joy without end.
THOMAS. O Judah, Judah, leave thy belief;
    His heart torn in pieces
        I saw.
    Notwithstanding what any man may say,
    That same body will remain;
        It has not risen.
ANDREW. Peace, Thomas, and say not a word;
    Very truly our dear Lord
        Is risen again.
    Surely too much thou hast disbelieved,
    For Mary has spoken
        With him to-day.
THOMAS. Thou art a fool, Andrew;
    The girl has told a lie,
        Do not think otherwise.
    That he ever rose again
    I will not believe it.

As long as I am alive.
MARY MAGDALENE. I have not said an untrue word;
   For to me all his wounds
     He shewed.
   And to that I will
   Bear witness at all times,
     That the tale is true.

[*Here let* THOMAS *and* MARY MAGDALENE *go down.*]

THOMAS. Notwithstanding vain words,
   I do not believe thee; thou failest
     To make me believe.
   Though thou dost chatter so much,
   Any thing from thee regards me not,
     Though thou be busy.
MARY MAGDALENE. I tell thee the truth;
   The angel said to us,
     Surely at the tomb,
   That he was risen up,
   And was gone to the bright heaven,
     With many angels.
THOMAS. Peace, chattering woman, say no more;
   I will not believe thee,
     That is gone to heaven.
   The body, which I saw dead,—
   Great are my anxieties
      After it.
MARY MAGDALENE. Surely Mary, mother of James,
   And Mary Salome,
     Will witness to me;
   Like as I saw,
   So I tell the tale to thee;
     Do believe it.
THOMAS. Never can it go into my heart,
   That the body dead before us
     Should rise again;
   When I think on his passion,
   Grief takes me immediately
     For him, woe is me!
MARY MAGDALENE. There is to me wonder of thee,
   That thy heart is so hard,
     Thou believest it not.
   If thou doest not believe it,
   Never shalt thou come to the joy

Surely which is in heaven.

THOMAS. Silence thou, now, for shame;
   With Jesus thou hast no secrets:
      Surely not! I believe
   Thou art a sinner, without a mistake;
   The greatest that was in the country
      By every body thou wast called.

MARY MAGDALENE. I have been a sinner;
   I have sinned wondrous much;
   On Jesus I cried,
      That he would forgive me my trespass;
   And he said to me,
   Thy sin is forgiven to thee,
   Through thy faith thou art saved:
      Now no more, do not sin.
      Thomas, thou art very stupid,
   Because thou wilt not believe
   The Lord to have risen
      Easter-day morning.
   Who believes not shall not be saved,
   Nor with God shall he dwell,
   And for that, I pray thee,
      Believe in time.

THOMAS. Hold thy prate, nor be busy,
   For I will not believe thee;
   The body was seen by me
      Fastened on the cross with nails;
   With a sharp spear they pierced him,
   So that it passed through the heart;
   To the earth the blood fell,
   And made him soon dead.
   That body cannot live,
   Nor rise up again,
      Surely, thou woman.
   There is not any man of this world
   Who shall make me now
      Believe otherwise.

MARY MAGDALENE. Thomas, thou art mad,
   And in madness lost;
      Evil it is with me now.
   I advise thee believe,
   And if thou dost not, seriously,
      Thou shalt have sharp repentance.

THOMAS. With you since there is no peace,
   From you I will go

My ways in the country.
Are ye not now fools?
So God help me,
 I love not lies.

[*Then* JESUS *comes to the apostles, and says (in Galilee, the doors
 being closed, he kisses them):*]

JESUS. The peace of God, O apostles!
 I, Christ, to rise from the tomb,
  Believe well;
 For certainly as many as believe it,
 And are faithfully baptized,
  Shall be saved.
PETER. O dear Lord, happy is my lot
 To see thee risen again,
  Jesus, though I denied thee.
 Abundant mercy, I pray,
 As the Jews are always
  Here laying snares for us.
  Jesus, Lord of heaven and earth,
 And Saviour to us also,
 Pardon me my trespass,
  For great are my sorrows.
 For sharp repentance falls on me
 For denying thee: now
 Mercy I pray at all times,
  Certainly, with full heart.
JESUS. Peter, pardon thou shalt get,
 For thy repentance is perfect,
  Through the Holy Ghost.
 Like as I redeemed thee dearly,
 Strengthen also thy brethren
  In full belief.
JOHN. O Lord, I am glad
 That thou wouldst come with us
  Hither, for our joy;
 That I will say likewise,
 We are, through great longing,
  After thee pining.
JESUS. From you I go to my country;
 At the right side of God the Father,
 I shall sit.
 To strengthen you in belief,
 To you the comfort of the Holy Ghost

I shall send.

JAMES THE GREATER. Lord, it is wonderful;
    When thou comest, Jesus powerful,
        To look at us,
    And to speak peace to us,
    Though they were fast, thou didst open
        Our doors.

[*Here* JESUS *goes away from the apostles.*]

He is the Lord of power,
And he has purchased with his blood
    The people of the world;
That Jesus Christ is risen again,—
A day is coming that shall tell
    All them that do believe it not!

The Wakefield Pageant of the Harrowing of Hell

OR, EXTRACTION OF SOULS FROM HELL

CHARACTERS

JESUS
ADAM
EVE
SIMEON
JOHN THE BAPTIST
MOSES
ESAIAS
DAVID
RIBALD
BEELZEBUB
SATHANAS

THE HARROWING OF HELL

EXTRACTIO ANIMARUM

AB INFERNO

[*The Extraction of Souls from Hell.*]

JESUS. My fader[414] me from blys has send
    Till's erthe for mankynde sake,
    Adam mys[415] for to amend,
    My deth nede must I take:

    I dwellyd ther thyrty yeres and two,
    And som dele more, the sothe to say,[416]
    In anger, pyne, and mekylle wo,
    I dyde on cros this day.

    Therefor tille helle now wille I go,
    To chalange[417] that is myne,
    Adam, Eve, and othere mo,
    Thay shalle no longer dwelle in pyne;

---

[414] father.
[415] Adam's miss, or fall.
[416] Sooth to say to thee.
[417] rescue.

The feynde[418] theym wan withe trayn,[419]
Thrughe fraude of earthly fode,[420]
I have theym boght agan
With shedyng of my blode.

And now I wille that stede[421] restore,
Whiche the feynde felle from for syn,
Som tokyn wille I send before,
Withe myrthe to gar[422] thare gammes begyn.

A light I wille thay have,
To know I wille com sone;
My body shalle abyde in grave
Tille alle this dede be done.

ADAM. My brether, herkyn unto me here,
More hope of helth never we had,
Four thousand and six hundred yere
Have we bene in darknes stad;[423]

Now se I tokyns of solace sere,[424]
A gloryous gleme to make us glad,
Wherthrughe I hope that help is nere,
That sone shalle slake[425] oure sorrowes sad.

EVE. Adam, my husband heynd,[426]
This menys solace certan,
Siche lighte can on us leynd[427]
In paradyse fulle playn.

ISAIAS. Adam, through thi syn
Here were we put to dwelle,
This wykyd place within,
The name of it is helle;

---

[418] fiend.
[419] betraying.
[420] earthly food—the apple.
[421] stead, state.
[422] make.
[423] stayed, kept.
[424] sure.
[425] slake thirst, lessen (or as in "slack a fire").
[426] gentle, gracious.
[427] linger.

Here paynes shalle never blyn[428]
That wykyd ar and felle,
Love, that lord, withe wyn
His lyfe for us wold selle.

[*Et cantent omnes "Salvator mundi" primum versum.*[429]]

Adam, thou welle understand,
I am Isaias, so Crist me kende,[430]
I spake of folk in darknes walkand,[431]
I saide a light shuld on them lende;

This light is alle from Crist commande,
That he tille us has hethir sende,
Thus is my poynt proved in hand,
As I before to fold[432] it kende.

SIMEON. So may I telle of farlys feylle,[433]
For in the tempylle his freyndes me fande,
Me thoght dayntethe[434] with hym to deylle,
I halsyd[435] hym homely with my hand,

I saide, Lord, let thi servandes leylle[436]
Pas in peasse to lyf lastande,[437]
Now that myn eeyn has sene thyn hele[438]
No longer lyst[439] I lyf in lande.

This light thou has purvayde
For theym that lyf in lede,[440]
That I before of the have saide
I se it is fulfillyd in dede.

---

[428] cease, leave.
[429] And all sing, Salvator Mundi, 1st ver.
[430] kenn'd, knew.
[431] walking.
[432] on earth.
[433] wonders many.
[434] deigneth, dignity.
[435] fondled.
[436] leal, true.
[437] lasting life.
[438] hal, salvation.
[439] list I, care I, to live.
[440] live in man, man's form.

JOHANNES BAPTISTA. As a voice cryand I kend[441]
    The wayes of Crist, as I welle can,
    I baptisid hym with bothe myn hende
    In the water of flume[442] Jordan;

    The Holy Gost from heven discende
    As a white dowfe downe on me than,
    The Fader voyce, oure myrthes to amende,
    Was made to me lyke as a man;[443]

    "Yond is my son," he saide,
    "And whiche pleasses me fulle welle,"
    His light is on us layde,
    And commys oure karys to kele.[444]

MOYSES. Now this same nyght lernyng have I,
    To me, Moyses, he shewid his myght,
    And also to another one, Hely,[445]
    Where we stud on a hille on hyght,

    As whyte as snaw was his body,
    His face was like the son for bright,
    No man on mold[446] was so mighty
    Grathly[447] durst loke agans[448] that light,

    And that same lighte here se I now
    Shynyng on us, certayn,
    Wherethrughe truly I trow
    That we shalle sone pas fro this payn.

RYBALD. Sen fyrst that helle was mayde and I was put therin
    Siche sorow never ere I had, nor hard I siche a dyn,[449]
    My hart begynnys to brade,[450] my wytt waxys thyn,[451]
    I drede we can not be glad, thise saules mon fro us twyn;[452]

---

[441] declared.
[442] flumen,—flood, river.
[443] The Father's voice was made like a man's.
[444] our cares to cool, cure, allay.
[445] Elias.
[446] earth.
[447] confidently.
[448] against.
[449] din, noise.
[450] to swell.
[451] my wit waxes thin.
[452] these souls men from us twine, divide.

How, Belsabub! bynde thise boys, siche "Harow"[453]
was never hard in helle.

BELZABUB. Out, Rybald! thou rorest what is betyd? can thou oght telle?

RYBALD. Whi, herys[454] thou not this ugly noyse?
　　Thise lurdans[455] that in lymbo dwelle,
　　They make menyng[456] of many joyse,
　　And muster myrthes theym emelle.[457]

BELZABUB. Myrth? nay, nay! that poynt is past,
　　More hope of helthe shalle they never have.

RYBALD. They cry on Crist fulle fast,
　　And says he shalle thaym save.

BELZABUB. Yee, though he do not, I shalle,
　　For thay ar sparyd[458] in specyalle space,
　　Whils I am prynce and pryncypalle,
　　Thay shalle never pas out of this place;

　　Calle up Astarot[459] and Anaballe,
　　To gyf us counselle in this case;
　　Belle, Berith and Bellyalle[460]
　　To mar theym that siche mastry mase;[461]

　　Say to sir Satan oure syre,
　　And byd hym bryng also
　　Sir Lucyfer lufly of lyre.[462]

RYBALD. Alle redy, lord, I go.

JESUS. Attolite portas, principes vestras, et elevamini portœ
　　æternales, et introibit rex gloriæ.[463]

---

[453] harrow—hullaballoo.
[454] hearest.
[455] louts.
[456] mixture.
[457] amongst.
[458] sparrian, to shut, to bar; sparian, preserve.
[459] Ashtaroth.
[460] Baal, Beryth and Belial.
[461] makes.
[462] lovely of face.

RYBALD. Out, harro,[464] out!—what deville is he
    That callys hym kyng over us alle?
    Hark Belzabub, com ne,[465]
    For hedusly[466] I hard hym calle.

BELZABUB. Go spar the yates,[467] ylle mot thou the![468]
    And set the waches[469] on the walle,
    If that brodelle[470] come ne
    With us ay won[471] he shalle:

    And if he more calle or cry,
    To make us more debate,
    Lay on hym hardlly,
    And make hym go his gate.[472]

DAVID. Nay, withe hym may ye not fyght,
    For he is king and conqueroure,
    And of so mekille myght,
    And styf in every stoure;[473]

    Of hym commys alle this light
    That shynys in this bowre;
    He is fulle fers in fight,
    Worthi to wyn honoure.

BELZABUB. Honoure! harsto,[474] harlot, for what dede
    Alle erthly men to me ar thralle,[475]
    That lad that thou callys lord in lede[476]
    He had never harbor, house, ne halle;

    How, sir Sathanas, com nar
    And hark this cursid rowte!

---

[463] Lift your heads, oh ye gates, and be ye lift up, ye everlasting doors, and the King of Glory shall come in.

[464] help.

[465] nigh.

[466] hideously.

[467] bolt the gates.

[468] prosper.

[469] watch.

[470] wretch.

[471] dwell.

[472] go his way.

[473] sturdy in every fight.

[474] hearest thou?

[475] are in thrall.

[476] God-in-man.

SATHANAS. The dewille you alle to har![477]
    What ales the so to showte?[478]
    And see, if I com nar,
    Thy brayn bot I bryst owte.[479]

BELZABUB. Thou must com help to spar,[480]
    We ar beseged abowte.

SATHANAS. Besegyd aboute! whi, who durst be so bold
    For drede to make on us a fray?

BELZABUB. It is the Jew that Judas sold
    For to be dede this othere day.

SATHANAS. How, in tyme that tale was told,
    That trature travesses[481] us alle way;
    He shalle be here fulle hard in hold,
    Bot loke he pas not I the pray.

BELZABUB. Pas! nay, nay, he wille not weynde[482]
    From hens or it be war,[483]
    He shapys hym for to sheynd[484]
    Alle helle e'er he go far.

SATHANAS. Fy, faturs,[485] therof shalle he faylle,
    For alle his fare[486] I hym defy;
    I know his trantes[487] fro top to taylle,[488]
    He lyffes by gawdes[489] and glory.

---

[477] the devil harry you all.
[478] ails thee to shout so?
[479] thy brain, I burst not out.
[480] shut the gates.
[481] betrays.
[482] wend, go.
[483] or we'll know it.
[484] destroy.
[485] traitors.
[486] danger.
[487] tricks.
[488] his.
[489] gauds, showy deeds.

Therby he broght furthe of oure baylle[490]
The lathe[491] Lazare of Betany,
Bot to the Jues I gaf counsaylle
That thay shuld cause hym dy:

I entered there into Judas
That forward[492] to fulfylle,
Therfor his hyere[493] he has
Alle wayes to won here stylle.[494]

RYBALD. Sir Sathan, sen we here the say[495]
     Thou and the Jues were at assent,
     And wote,[496] he wan the Lazare away
     That unto us was taken to tent,[497]

     Hopys thou that thou mar hym may
     To muster[498] the malyce that he has ment?
     For and he refe[499] us now oure pray
     We wille ye witt e'er he is went.

SATHANAS. I byd the noght abaste[500]
     Bot boldly make you bowne,[501]
     Withe toyles that ye intraste,[502]
     And dyng[503] that dastard downe.

JESUS. Attolite portas, principes vestras, et elevamini portæ
     æternales, et introibit rex gloriæ.[504]

RYBALD. Outt, harro![505] what harlot is he
     That says his kyngdom shal be cryde?

---

[490] from our bale, destruction.
[491] hateful.
[492] agreement, or forward precaution, foreword, prearrange.
[493] his hire, reward.
[494] to dwell here still.
[495] since we hear thee say.
[496] know.
[497] taken in charge.
[498] frustrate.
[499] rive, take away.
[500] be nought abased.
[501] bound.
[502] truss up, entangle ("take in the toils").
[503] ding, knock.
[504] see p. 153.
[505] help.

DAVID. That may thou in sawter se,[506]
 For of this prynce thus err I saide;[507]

  I saide that he shuld breke
  Youre barres and bandes by name,[508]
  And of youre wareks take wreke;[509]
  Now shall thou se the same.

JESUS. Ye prynces of helle open youre yate,
 And let my folk furthe gone,
 A prynce of peasse shalle enter therat
 Wheder ye wille or none.

RYBALD. What art thou that spekys so?

JESUS. A kyng of blys that hight Jesus.

RYBALD. Yee hens fast I red[510] thou go,
 And melle[511] the not with us.

BELZABUB. Oure yates[512] I trow wille last,
 Thay ar so strong I weyn,[513]
 Bot if oure barres brast,
 For the, thay shalle not twyn.[514]

JESUS. This stede[515] shalle stande no longer stokyn;[516]
 Open up and let my pepille pas.

RYBALD. Out, harro![517] oure baylle is brokyn,[518]
 And brusten ar alle oure bandes of bras.

---

[506] see in the psalter.
[507] I always said.
[508] "be naame," a technical term for seizure of another's goods.
[509] make wreck of your works.
[510] advise.
[511] meddle.
[512] gates.
[513] ween.
[514] twine, part asunder.
[515] stead, place.
[516] closed, fast shut.
[517] help.
[518] bailey, outer gate.

BELZABUB. Harro! oure yates begyn to crak,
In sonder, I trow, thay go,
And helle, I trow, wille all to-shak;
Alas, what I am wo![519]

RYBALD. Lymbo is lorn, alas!
Sir Sathanas, com up!
This wark is wars[520] than it was.

SATHANAS. Yee, hangyd be thou on a cruke;[521]

Thefys, I bad ye shuld be bowne[522]
If he maide masters[523] more
To dyng[524] that dastard downe,
Sett[525] hym bothe sad and sore.

BELZABUB. "So sett hym sore" that is sone saide.
Com thou thi self and serve hym so;
We may not abyde his bytter bradye,[526]
He wold us mar and we were mo.[527]

SATHANAS. Fy, fature![528] wherfore were ye flayd?[529]
Have ye no force to flyt hym fro?
Loke in haste my gere be grayd,[530]
My self shalle to that gadlyng go.[531]

How, thou belamy, abyde,[532]
Withe alle thi boste and beyr,[533]
And telle me in this tyde
What masters[534] thou makes here.

---

[519] how am I woeful.
[520] worse.
[521] crook.
[522] ready.
[523] masteries.
[524] knock, strike, beset.
[525] Make him.
[526] stratagem, treachery.
[527] more, or stronger.
[528] traitor.
[529] afraid.
[530] my gear, weapons, be ready.
[531] gad-about, vagrant.
[532] Bel ami, fair friend.
[533] noise, hubbub.
[534] pain, afflict.

JESUS. I make no mastry bot for myne,
    I wille theym save, that shalle the sow,
    Thou has no powere theym to pyne,[535]
    Bot in my pryson for thare prow[536]

    Here have thay sojornyd,—not as thyne,
    Bot in thi wayrd,[537] thou wote as how.

SATHANAS. Why, where has thou hene ay syn[538]
    That never wold neghe[539] theym nere e'er now?

JESUS. Now is the tyme certan
    My Fader ordand herfor,[540]
    That they shuld pas fro payn
    In blys to dwelle for ever more.

SATHANAS. Thy fader knew I welle by syght,
    He was a wright his meett to wyn,[541]
    Mary, me mynnys,[542] thi moder hight,
    The utmast ende of alle thy kyn:

    Say who made the so mekille[543] of myght?

JESUS. Thou wykyd feynde lett be thi dy [n] ,
    My Fader wonnes[543] in heven on hight,
    In blys that never more shalle blyn:[544]
    I am his oonly son his forward[545] to fulfylle,
    Togeder wille we won, in sonder when we wylle.

SATHANAS. Goddes son! nay, then myght thou be glad
    For no catelle thurt the crave;[546]
    Bot thou has lyffed ay lyke a lad,
    In sorow, and as a sympille[547] knave.

---

[535] profit.
[536] ward, keeping.
[537] aye syne, ever since.
[538] go nigh.
[539] ordained heretofore.
[540] to get his meat, earn his bread.
[541] I mind, remember.
[542] mickle, much.
[543] lives.
[544] cease.
[545] prophecy.
[546] For no chattles need you crave (lack), or ask.

JESUS. That was for the hartly[548] luf I had
    Unto man's saulle, it for to save,
    And for to make thee masyd[549] and mad,
    And for that reson rufully to rafe.[550]

    My Godhede here I hyd
    In Mary, moder myne,
    Where it shalle never be kyd[551]
    To the, ne none of thyne.[552]

SATHANAS. How now? this wold I were told in towne,
    Thou says God is thi syre;
    I shalle the prove by good reson
    Thou moyttes[553] as man dos into myre.

    To breke thi byddyng they were fulle bowne,[554]
    And soon they wroght at my desyre,
    From paradise thou putt thym downe,
    In helle here to have thare hyre;[555]

    And thou thi self, by day and nyght,
    Taght[556] ever alle men emang,
    Ever to do reson and right,
    And here thou wyrkys[557] alle wrang.

JESUS. I wyrk no wrang, that shalle thou wytt.[558]
    If I my men fro wo wille wyn;[559]
    My prophettes playnly prechyd it,
    Alle the noytys[560] that I begyn;

---

[547] simple.
[548] hearty.
[549] amazed.
[550] rave.
[551] manifest, made known.
[552] to thee, nor none of thine.
[553] errest.
[554] ready.
[555] hire, reward.
[556] taught.
[557] workest.
[558] know.
[559] win, save (my men from woe).
[560] concerns, things of note.

They saide that I shud be that ilke
In helle where I shud entre in,
To save my servandes fro that pytt
Where dampynyd saullys[561] shalle syt for syn.

And ilke true prophete taylle[562]
Shalle be fulfillid in me;
I have thaym boght fro baylle,[563]
In blis now shalle thay be.

SATHANAS. Now since thou list to legge the lawes[564]
Thou shalbe tenyd or we twyn,[565]
For those that thou to witnes drawes
Fulle even agans the shalle begyn;

As Salaman saide in his sawes,[566]
Who that ones commys helle within
He shalle never owte, as clerkes knawes
Therfor, belamy, let be thy dyn.[567]

Job thi servande also
In his tyme can telle
That nawder freynde nor fo
Shalle fynde relese in helle.[568]

JESUS. He sayde fulle soythe, that shalle thou se,
In helle shalbe no relese,
Bot of that place then ment he
Where synfulle care shalle ever encrese.

In that baylle ay shalle thou be,
Where sorrowes seyr shalle never sesse[569]
And my folk that wer most fre[570]
Shalle pas unto the place of peasse;

---

561 damned souls.
562 true prophets' tale.
563 bale, destruction.
564 quote, or read, the laws.
565 convinced ere we part.
566 saws, proverbs.
567 din, noise.
568 neither friend nor foe shall find release in hell.
569 sorrows sore shall never cease.
570 noble.

For thay were here with my wille,
And so thay shalle furthe weynde,[571]
Thou shalle thi self fulfylle,
Ever wo withoutten ende.

SATHANAS. Whi, and wille thou take theym alle me fro?[572]
Then thynk me[573] thou ar unkynde;
Nay, I pray the do not so,
Umthynke[574] the better in thy mynde,

Or els let me with the go;
I pray the leyfe me not behynde.

JESUS. Nay, tratur, thou shalle won in wo,[575]
And tille a stake[576] I shalle the bynde.

SATHANAS. Now here I how thou menys[577] emang
With mesure and malyce for to melle,[578]
Bot sen thou says it shalbe lang,
Yit som let alle wayes with us dwelle.

JESUS. Yis, witt thou welle, els were greatt wrang,
Thou shalle have Caym[579] that slo Abelle,
And alle that hastes theym self to hang,
As dyd Judas and Architophelle;
And Daton and Abaron and alle of thare assent,[580]
Cursyd tyranttes ever ilkon[581] that me and myn tormente.

And alle that wille not lere[582] my law
That I have left in land for new[583]
That makes my commyng knaw,[584]
And alle my sacramentes persew;

---

[571] wend, go.
[572] take them all from me.
[573] methinks.
[574] bethink.
[575] dwell in woe.
[576] to a stake.
[577] moanest.
[578] with measure and malice (malice aforethought) to meddle.
[579] Cain.
[580] Dathan and Abiram, and all of their.
[581] each one.
[582] learn.
[583] henceforth.
[584] my coming known.

My deth, my rysyng, red by raw,[585]
Who trow thaym not thay ar untrewe,
Unto my dome[586] I shalle theym draw,
And juge thaym wars[587] then any Jew.
And thay that lyst to lere my law and lyf therby
Shalle never have harmes here, bot welth as is worthy.

SATHANAS. Now here my hand, I hold me payde,
    Thise poyntes ar playnly for my prow,[588]
    If this be trew as thou has saide
    We shalle have mo then we have now;

    Thise lawes that thou has late here laide
    I shalle thym lere not to alow,[589]
    If thay myn take[590] thay ar betraide,
    And I shalle turne thym tytte I trow.[591]

    I shalle walk eest, I shalle walk west,
    And gar theym wyrk welle war.[592]

JESUS. Nay feynde, thou shalbe feste,[593]
    That thou shalle flyt no far.[594]

SATHANAS. Feste? fy! that were a wykyd treson!
    Belamy, thou shalle be smytt.[595]

JESUS. Deville, I commaunde the to go downe
    Into thi sete where thou shalle syt.

SATHANAS. Alas! for doylle[596] and care,
    I synk into helle pyt.

---

[585] by row, line by line, all in order.
[586] doom.
[587] judge them worse.
[588] profit.
[589] teach them not to permit.
[590] follow mine (my laws).
[591] turn them to it, I trow.
[592] and make them grow well aware.
[593] fast-bound.
[594] fly not far.
[595] Bel ami (fair friend), thou shalt be smitten down.
[596] grief.

RYBALD. Sir Sathanas, so saide I are,[597]
    Now shalle thou have a fytt.

JESUS. Com now furthe, my childer alle,
    I forgyf you youre mys;[598]
    Withe me now go ye shalle
    To joy and endles blys.

ADAM. Lord, thou art fulle mekylle of myght,[599]
    That mekys thi self on this manere,
    To help us alle as thou had us hight,
    When bothe frofett I and my fere;[600]

    Here have we dwelt withoutten light
    Four thousand and six hundreth yere,
    Now se we by this solempne sight
    How that mercy makes us dere.

EVA. Lord, we were worthy more tornamentes[601] to tast,[602]
    Thou help us lord of thy mercy, as thou of myght is mast.[603]

JOHANNES. Lord, I love the inwardly,
    That me wold make thi messyngere,
    Thi commyng in erthe to cry,
    And teche thi fayth to folk in fere;[604]

    Sythen before the forto dy,[605]
    To bryng theym bodword[606] that be here,
    How thay shuld have thi help in hy,
    Now se I alle those poyntes appere.

MOYSES. David, thi prophette trew,
    Of tymes told unto us;
    Of thi commyng he knew,
    And saide it shuld be thus.

---

[597] So said I e'er,—always.
[598] sins.
[599] mickle, great of might.
[600] companion.
[601] torments.
[602] taste.
[603] master.
[604] in fear.
[605] since before thee.
[606] bode-word; (foreboding, forewarning).

DAVID. As I said ere yit say I so,
　　Ne derelinquas, domine,
　　Animam meam in inferno;[607]
　　Leyfe never my saulle, Lord, after the,

　　In depe helle whedur[608] dampned shalle go
　　Suffre thou never thi sayntes to se
　　The sorrow of thaym that won in wo,[609]
　　Ay, fulle of fylthe, and may not fle.[610]

MOYSES. Make myrthe bothe more and les,
　　And love oure lord we may,
　　That has broght us fro bytternes
　　In blys to abyde for ay.

YSAIAS. Therfor now let us syng
　　To love oure lord Jesus,
　　Unto his blys he wille us bryng,
　　Te Deum laudamus.

---

[607] "Thou didst not leave, oh Lord, my soul in hell!"

[608] Whither the damned shall go.

[609] live in woe.

[610] flee, escape.

The Interlude of "God's Promises"

BY JOHN BALE

CHARACTERS

PATER CŒLESTIS THE HEAVENLY FATHER
ADAM PRIMUS HOMO ADAM, THE FIRST MAN
JUSTUS NOAH JUST NOAH
ABRAHAM FIDELIS FAITHFUL ABRAHAM
MOSES SANCTUS SAINT MOSES
DAVID REX PIUS THE PIOUS KING, DAVID
ESAIAS PROPHETA THE PROPHET ISAIAH
BALEUS PROLOCUTOR JOHN BALE, WHO SPEAKS THE PROLOGUE

GOD'S PROMISES

A Tragedy or interlude manifesting the chief promises of God unto man by all ages in the old law, from the Fall of Adam to the Incarnation of the Lord Jesus Christ. Compiled by John Bale, (Anno Domini MDXXXVIII.).

BALEUS PROLOCUTOR. If profit may grow, most Christian audience,
By knowledge of things which are but transitory,
And here for a time, of much more congruence,
Advantage might spring, by the search of causes heavenly,
As those matters are that the gospel specify.
Without whose knowledge no man to the truth can fall,
Nor ever attain to the life perpetual,
　　For he that knoweth not the living God eternal
The Father, the Son and also the Holy Ghost,
And what Christ suffered for redemption of us all,
What he commanded, and taught in every coast,
And what he forbode, that man must needs be lost,
And clean secluded, from the faithful chosen sort,
In the Heavens above, to his most high discomfort.
　　You therefore, good friends, I lovingly exhort,
To weigh such matters as will be uttered here,
Of whom ye may look to have no trifling sport
In fantasies feigned, nor such-like gaudy gear,
But the things that shall your inward stomach cheer.
To rejoice in God for your justification,
And alone in Christ to hope for your salvation.
　　Yea first ye shall have the eternal generation

Of Christ, like as John in his first chapter write,
And consequently of man the first creation
The abuse and fall, through his first oversight,
And the rise-again through God's high grace and might;
By promises first which shall be declared all:
Then by his own Son, the worker principal.

 After that, Adam bewaileth here his fall;
God will shew mercy to every generation,
And to his kingdom of his great goodness call
His elected spouse, or faithful congregation,
As shall appear by open protestation,
Which from Christ's birth shall to his death conclude:
They come, that thereof will shew the certitude.

ACT I

ADAM THE FIRST MAN

PATER CŒLESTIS. In the beginning before the heavens were create,
 In me and of me was my Son sempiternal
 With the Holy Ghost, in one degree or estate
 Of the high Godhead, to me the Father coequal
 And this my Son was with me one God essential
 Without separation at any time from me.
 True God he is of equal dignity.
 Since the beginning my Son hath ever been
 Joined with his father in one essential being.
 All things were create by him in each degree,
 In heaven and earth and have their diverse working:
 Without his power, was never made any thing
 That was wrought; but through his ordinance
 Each have his strength, and whole continuance.

 In him is the life and the just recoverance
 For Adam and his, which nought but death deserved.
 And this life to men is an high perseverance
 Or a light of faith, whereby they shall be saved.
 And this light shall shine among the people darkened
 With unfaithfulness. Yet shall they not with him take
 But of wilful heart his liberal grace forsake.
 Which will compel me against man for to make
 In my displeasure, and send plagues of correction
 Most grievous and sharp, his wanton lusts to slake,
 By water and fire, by sickness and infection
 Of pestilent sores, molesting his complexion;
 By troublous war, by dearth and painful scarceness,

And after this life by an extreme heaviness.
I will first begin with Adam for his lewdness
Which for an apple neglected my commandment.
He shall continue in labour for his rashness,
His only sweat shall provide his food and raiment:
Yea, yet must he have a greater punishment,
Most terrible death shall bring him to his end
To teach him how he his Lord God shall offend.

[*Here* ADAM *falls headlong upon the earth and after rolling over
four times, at last gets up.*]

ADAM. Merciful Father, thy pitiful grace extend
    To me, careful wretch, which have me sore abused
    Thy precept breaking, O Lord, I mean to amend,
    If now thy great goodness would have me excused,
    Most heavenly Maker, let me not be refused,
    Nor cast from thy sight for one poor sinful crime;
    Alas! I am frail, my whole kind is but slime.
PATER CŒLESTIS. I wot it is so, yet art thou no less faulty
    Than thou hadst been made of matter much more worthy.
    I gave thee reason and wit to understand
    The good from the evil, and not to take on hand
    Of a brainless mind, the thing which I forbade thee.
ADAM. Such heavy fortune hath chiefly chanced me
    For that I was left to mine own liberty.
PATER CŒLESTIS. Then thou are blameless, and the fault thou layest to
me?
ADAM. Nay, all I ascribe to my own imbecility.
    No fault in thee Lord but in my infirmity,
    And want of respect in such gifts as thou gavest me.
PATER CŒLESTIS. For that I put thee at thine own liberty,
    Thou oughtest my goodness to have in more regard.
ADAM. Avoid it I cannot, thou layest it to me so hard.
    Lord, now I perceive what power is in man,
    And strength of himself, when thy sweet grace is absent,
    He must needs but fall, do he the best he can,
    And endanger himself, as appeareth evident;
    For I sinned not so long as thou wert present;
    But when thou wert gone, I fell to sin by and by,
    And thee displeased. Good Lord, I ask thee mercy.
PATER CŒLESTIS. Thou shalt die for it and all thy posterity.
ADAM. For one fault, good Lord, avenge not thyself on me,
    Who am but a worm, or a fleshly vanity.
PATER CŒLESTIS. I say thou shalt die with thy whole posterity.

ADAM. Yet mercy, sweet Lord, if any mercy may be.

PATER CŒLESTIS. I am immutable, I may change no decree.
 Thou shalt die, I say, without any remedy.

ADAM. Yet gracious Father, extend to me thy mercy,
 And throw not away the work which thou hast create
 To thine own image, but avert from me thy hate.

PATER CŒLESTIS. But art thou sorry from bottom of thy heart?

ADAM. Thy displeasure is to me most heavy smart.

PATER CŒLESTIS. Then will I tell thee what thou shalt stick unto,
 Life to recover, and my good favour also.

ADAM. Tell it me, sweet Lord, that I may thereafter go.

PATER CŒLESTIS. This is my covenant to thee and all thy offspring.
 For that thou hast been deceived by the serpent,
 I will put hatred betwixt him for his doing
 And the woman kind. They shall hereafter dissent;
 His seed with her seed shall never have agreement;
 Her seed shall press down his head unto the ground,
 Slay his suggestions, and his whole power confound.
  Cleave to this promise with all thy inward power,
 Firmly enclose it in thy remembrance fast,
 Fold it in thy faith with full hope, day and hour,
 And thy salvation it will be at the last.
 That seed shall clear thee of all thy wickedness past,
 And procure thy peace, with most high grace in my sight,
 See thou trust to it and hold not the matter light.

ADAM. Sweet lord, the promise that thyself here hath made me,
 Of thy mere goodness and not of my deserving,
 In my faith I trust shall so established be,
 By help of thy grace, that it shall be remaining
 So long as I shall have here continuing;
 And shew it I will to my posterity
 That they in like case have thereby felicity.

PATER CŒLESTIS. For a closing up, take yet one sentence with thee.

ADAM. At thy pleasure, Lord, all things might ever be.

PATER CŒLESTIS. For that my promise may have the deeper effect
 In the faith of thee and all thy generation,
 Take this sign with it, as a seal thereto connect.
 Creep shall the serpent, for his abomination,
 The woman shall sorrow in painful propagation.
 Like as thou shalt find this true in outward working,
 So think the other, though it be a hidden thing.

ADAM. Incessant praising to thee most heavenly lord
 For this thy succour, and undeserved kindness,
 Thou bindest me in heart thy gracious gifts to record,
 And to bear in mind, now after my heaviness,

The bruit of thy name, with inward joy and gladness.
Thou disdainest not, as well appeareth this day,
To fetch to thy fold thy first sheep going astray.

    Most mighty Maker, thou castest not yet away
Thy sinful servant, which hath done most offence.
It is not thy mind for ever I should decay,
But thou reservest me, of thy benevolence,
And hast provided for me a recompence,
By thy appointment, like as I have received
In thy strong promise here openly pronounced.

    This goodness, dear Lord, is of me undeserved,
I so declining from thy first institution,
At so light motions. To one that thus hath swerved,
What a lord art thou, to give such retribution!
I, damnable wretch, deserved execution
Of terrible death, without all remedy,
And to be put out of all good memory.
I am enforced to rejoice here inwardly,
An imp though I be of hell, death and damnation,
Through my own working: for I consider thy mercy
And pitiful mind for my whole generation.
It is thou, sweet Lord, that workest my salvation,
And my recovery. Therefore of a congruence
From hence thou must have my heart and obedience.
Though I be mortal, by reason of my offence,
And shall die the death like as God hath appointed:
Of this I am sure, through his high influence,
At a certain day again to be revived.
From ground of my heart this shall not be removed,
I have it in faith and therefore I will sing
This anthem to him that my salvation shall bring.

[*Then with sonorous voice, on his bent knees, he begins an
    antiphon, "O Sapientia," which the chorus follows with
    instruments, as it removes from the stage. Or else in the same
    it may thus be sung in English:*]

    O Eternal Sapience, that proceedest from the mouth of the
highest, reaching forth with a great power from the beginning to
the end, with heavenly sweetness disposing all creatures, come
now and instruct us the true way of thy godly prudence.

Act II

Noah the Just

PATER CŒLESTIS. I have been moved to strike man diversely,
    Since I left Adam in this same earthly mansion;
    For why? He hath done to me displeasures many,
    And will not amend his life in any condition:
    No respect hath he to my word nor monition,
    But what doth him lust, without discreet advisement,
    And will in nowise take mine advertisement.
      Cain hath slain Abel, his brother, an innocent,
    Whose blood from the earth doth call to me for vengeance:
    My children with men's so carnally consent,
    That their vain working is unto me much grievance:
    Mankind is but flesh in his whole dalliance.
    All vice increaseth in him continually,
    Nothing he regardeth to walk unto my glory.
      My heart abhorreth his wilful misery,
    His cancred malice, his cursed covetousness,
    His lusts lecherous, his vengeable tyranny,
    Unmerciful murder and other ungodliness.
    I will destroy him for his outrageousness,
    And not him only, but all that on earth do stir,
    For it repenteth me that ever I made them here.
NOAH. Most gentle Maker, with his frailness somewhat bear,
    Man is thy creature, thyself cannot say nay.
    Though thou punish him to put him somewhat in fear,
    His fault to acknowledge, yet seek not his decay.
    Thou mayest reclaim him, though he goeth now astray,
    And bring him again, of thy abundant grace,
    To the fold of faith, he acknowledging his trespass.
PATER CŒLESTIS. Thou knowest I have given to him convenient space,
    With lawful warnings, yet he amendeth in no place.
    The natural laws, which I wrote in his heart,
    He hath outraced, all goodness putting apart:
    Of health the covenant, which I to Adam made,
    He regardeth not, but walketh a damnable trade.
NOAH. All this is true, Lord, I cannot thy words reprove,
    Let his weakness yet thy merciful goodness move.
PATER CŒLESTIS. No weakness is it, but wilful working all,
    That reigneth in man through mind diabolical.
    He shall have therefore like as he hath deserved.
NOAH. Lose him not yet, Lord, though he has deeply swerved.

I know thy mercy is far above his rudeness,
Being infinite, as all other things are in thee.
His folly therefore now pardon of thy goodness,
And measure it not beyond thy godly pity.
Esteem not his fault farther than help may be,
But grant him thy grace, as he offendeth so deeply,
Thee to remember, and abhor his misery.
Of all goodness, Lord, remember thy great mercy,
To Adam and Eve, breaking thy first commandment.
Them thou relievedst with thy sweet promise heavenly,
Sinful though they were, and their lives negligent.
I know that mercy with thee is permanent,
And will be ever so long as the world endure:
Then close not thy hand from man, which is thy creature.
　　Being thy subject he is underneath thy cure,
Correct him thou mayest and so bring him to grace.
All lieth in thy hands, to leave or to allure,
Bitter death to give, or grant most sovereign solace.
Utterly from man avert not then thy face;
But let him savour thy sweet benevolence
Somewhat, though he feel thy hand for his offence.

PATER CŒLESTIS. My true servant Noah, thy righteousness doth move
　　me
　　Somewhat to reserve for man's posterity.
　　Though I drown the world, yet will I save the lives
　　Of thee and thy wife, thy three sons and their wives,
　　And of each kind two, to maintain you hereafter.
NOAH. Blessed be thy name, most mighty merciful Maker,
　　With thee to dispute, it were inconvenient.
PATER CŒLESTIS. Why dost thou say so? Be bold to speak thy intent.
NOAH. Shall the other die without any remedy?
PATER CŒLESTIS. I will drown them all, for their wilful wicked folly
　　That man hereafter thereby may know my power,
　　And fear to offend my goodness day and hour.
NOAH. As thy pleasure is, so might it always be,
　　For my health thou art and soul's felicity.
PATER CŒLESTIS. After that this flood have had his raging passage
　　This shall be to thee my covenant everlasting.
　　The seas and waters so far never more shall rage,
　　As all flesh to drown, I will so temper their working;
　　This sign will I add also, to confirm the thing,
　　In the clouds above, as a seal or token clear,
　　For safeguard of man, my rainbow shall appear.
　　　Take thou this covenant for an earnest confirmation
　　Of my former promise to Adam's generation.

NOAH. I will, blessed Lord, with my whole heart and mind.
PATER CŒLESTIS. Farewell then, just Noah, here leave I thee behind,
NOAH. Most mighty Maker, ere I from hence depart,
    I must give thee praise from the bottom of my heart.
    Whom may we thank, Lord, for our health and salvation
    But thy great mercy and goodness undeserved?
    Thy promise, in faith, is our justification,
    As it was Adam's when his heart therein rested,
    And as it was theirs which therein also trusted.
    This faith was grounded in Adam's memory,
    And clearly declared in Abel's innocency.
    Faith in that promise old Adam did justify,
    In that promise faith made Eve to prophecy.
    Faith in that promise proved Abel innocent,
    In that promise faith made Seth full obedient.
    That faith taught Enoch on God's name first to call,
    And made Methuselah the oldest man of all.
    That faith brought Enoch to so high exercise,
    That God took him up with him into Paradise.
    Of that faith the want made Cain to hate the good,
    And all his offspring to perish in the flood.
    Faith in that promise preserved both me and mine:
    So will it all them which follow the same line.
    Not only this gift thou hast given me, sweet Lord,
    But with it also thine everlasting covenant
    Of trust forever, thy rainbow bearing record,
    Never more to drown the world by flood inconstant;
    Alack! I cannot to thee give praise condign,
    Yet will I sing here with heart meek and benign.

[*Then in a great voice he begins an antiphon, "O Oriens Splendor," falling upon his knees while the chorus follows with instruments, as before.*]

O most orient clearness, and light shining of the sempiternal brightness! O clear sun of justice and heavenly righteousness, come hither and illuminate the prisoner sitting in the dark prison and shadow of Eternal Death.

ACT III

OF FAITHFUL ABRAHAM

PATER CŒLESTIS. Mine high displeasure must needs return to man,
    Considering the sin that he doth day by day;
    For neither kindness nor extreme handling can
    Make him to know me by any faithful way,
    But still in mischief he walketh to his decay.
    If he do not soon his wickedness consider,
    He is like, doubtless, to perish altogether.
      In my sight, he is more venym[611] than the spider,
    Through such abuses as he hath exercised,
    From the time of Noah to this same season hither.
    An uncomely act without shame Ham commysed.[612]
    When he of his father the secret parts revealed.
    In like case Nimrod against me wrought abusion
    As he raised up the castle of confusion.
      Mirus hath also, and all by the devil's illusion
    Through image-making, up raised idolatry,
    Me to dishonour. And now in the conclusion
    The vile Sodomites live so unnaturally
    That their sin vengeance asketh continually,
    For my covenant's sake, I will not drown with water,
    Yet shall I visit their sins with other matter.
ABRAHAM. Yet, merciful Lord, thy graciousness remember
    To Adam and Noah, both in thy word and promise:
    And lose not the souls of men in so great number
    But save thine own work, of thy most discreet goodness.
    I wot thy mercies are plentiful and earnest,
    Never can they die nor fail, thyself enduring,
    This hath faith fixed fast in my understanding.
PATER CŒLESTIS. Abraham my servant, for thy most faithful meaning,
    Both thou and thy stock shall have my plenteous blessing.
    When the unfaithful, under my curse evermore,
    For their vain working, shall rue their wickedness sore.
ABRAHAM. Tell me, blessed Lord, where will thy great malice light?
    My hope is, all flesh shall not perish in thy sight.
PATER CŒLESTIS. No truly, Abraham, thou chancest upon the right,
    The thing I shall do I will not hide from thee,
    Whom I have blessed for thy true fidelity:

---

[611] venomous.
[612] committed.

For I know thou wilt cause both thy children and servants,
In my ways to walk, and trust unto my covenants,
That I may perform with thee my earnest promise.
ABRAHAM. All that I will do, by assistance of thy goodness.
PATER CŒLESTIS. From Sodom and Gomor the abominations call
For my great vengeance, which will upon them fall,
Wild fire and brimstone shall light upon them all.
ABRAHAM. Pitiful Maker, though they have kindled thy fury,
Cast not away yet the just sort with the ungodly.
Peradventure there may be fifty righteous persons
Within those cities, wilt thou lose them all at once,
And not spare the place for those fifty righteous' sake
Be it far from thee such rigour to undertake.
    I hope there is not in thee so cruel hardness,
As to cast away the just men with the reckless,
And so to destroy the good with the ungodly:
In the judge of all: be never such a fury.
PATER CŒLESTIS. At Sodom, if I may find just persons fifty,
The place will I spare for their sakes verily.
ABRAHAM. I take upon me to speak here in thy presence,
More than becomes me, lord, pardon my negligence:
I am but ashes and were loth thee to offend.
PATER CŒLESTIS. Say forth, good Abraham, for ill dost thou not intend.
ABRAHAM. Haply there may be five less in the same number,
For thy sake I hope thou wilt not the rest accombre.[613]
PATER CŒLESTIS. If I among them might find but five and forty
Them would I not lose for that just company.
ABRAHAM. What if the city may forty righteous make?
PATER CŒLESTIS. Then will I pardon it for those same forty's sake.
ABRAHAM. Be not angry, Lord, though I speak undiscreetly.
PATER CŒLESTIS. Utter thy whole mind and spare me not hardly.
ABRAHAM. Peradventure there may be thirty found among them.
PATER CŒLESTIS. May I find thirty, I will nothing do unto them.
ABRAHAM. I take upon me too much, Lord, in thy sight.
PATER CŒLESTIS. No, no, good Abraham, for I know thy faith is right.
ABRAHAM. No less, I suppose, than twenty can it have.
PATER CŒLESTIS. Could I find twenty, that city would I save.
ABRAHAM. Once yet will I speak my mind, and then no more.
PATER CŒLESTIS. Spare not to utter so much as thou hast in store.
ABRAHAM. And what if there might be ten good creatures found?
PATER CŒLESTIS. The rest for their sakes might so be safe and sound,
And not destroyed for their abomination.
ABRAHAM. O merciful Maker, much is thy toleration

---

[613] overwhelm.

And sufferance of sin: I see it now indeed;
Vouchsafe yet of favour out of those cities to lead
Those that be faithful, though their flock be but small.
PATER CŒLESTIS. Lot and his household, I will deliver all,
For righteousness sake, which is of me and not them.
ABRAHAM. Great are thy graces in the generation of Shem.
PATER CŒLESTIS. Well, Abraham, well, for thy true faithfulness
Now will I give thee my covenant or third promise.
Look thou believe it as thou covetest righteousness.
ABRAHAM. Lord, so regard me as I receive it with gladness.
PATER CŒLESTIS. Of many peoples the father I will make thee,
All generations in thy seed shall be blessed:
As the stars of heaven, so shall thy kindred be;
And by the same seed the world shall be redressed
In circumcision shall this thing be expressed,
As in a sure seal, to prove my promise true,
Print this in thy faith, and it shall thy soul renew.
ABRAHAM. I will not one jot, Lord, from thy will dissent
But to thy pleasure be always obedient,
Thy laws to fulfil, and most precious commandment.
PATER CŒLESTIS. Farewell, Abraham, for here in place I leave thee.
ABRAHAM. Thanks will I render, like as it shall behove me.
Everlasting praise to thy most glorious name,
Which savedst Adam through faith in thy sweet promise
Of the woman's seed, and now confirmest the same
In the seed of me. Forsooth great is thy goodness.
I cannot perceive but that thy mercy is endless.
To such as fear thee, in every generation,
For it endureth without abbreviation.
    This have I printed in deep consideration,
No worldly matter can rase it out of mind.
For once it will be the final restoration
Of Adam and Eve, and other that hath sinned;
Yea, the sure health and race of mankind.
Help have the faithful thereof, though they be infect;
They, condemnation, where as it is reject.
    Merciful Maker, my crabbed voice direct,
That it may break out in some sweet praise to thee;
And suffer me not thy due lauds to neglect,
But let me show forth thy commendations free.
Stop not my windpipes, but give them liberty,
To sound to thy name, which is most gracious,
And in it rejoice with heart melodious.

[*Then in a loud voice he begins the antiphon, "O rex gentium," the chorus following the same with instruments.*]

O most mighty Governor of thy people, and in heart most desired, the hard rock and the true corner-stone, that of two maketh one, uniting the Jews with the Gentiles in one church, come now and relieve mankind, whom thou hast formed of the vile earth.

ACT IV

MOSES SANCTUS

PATER CŒLESTIS. Still so increaseth the wickedness of man,
    That I am moved with plagues him to confound.
    His weakness to aid, I do the best I can,
    Yet he regardeth me no more than doth a hound,
    My word and promise in his faith taketh no ground;
    He will so long walk in his own lusts at large,
    That naught he shall find his folly to discharge.
      Since Abraham's time, which was my true elect,
    Ishmael have I found both wicked, fierce and cruel:
    And Esau in mind with hateful murder infect.
    The sons of Jacob to lusts unnatural fell,
    And into Egypt did they their brother sell.
    Laban to idols gave faithful reverence,
    Dinah was corrupt through Shechem's violence.
      Reuben abused his father's concubine,
    Judah got children of his own daughter-in-law:
    Yea, she in my sight went after a wicked line.
    His seed Onan spilt, his brother's name to withdraw.
    Achan lived here without all godly awe.
    And now the children of Israel abuse my power
    In so vile manner that they move me every hour.
MOSES. Pacify thy wrath, sweet Lord, I thee desire,
    As thou art gentle, benign, and patient,
    Lose not that people in fierceness of thine ire
    For whom thou hast shewed such tokens evident,
    Converting this rod into a lively serpent,
    And the same serpent into this rod again,
    Thy wonderful power declaring very plain.
      For their sakes also puttest Pharaoh to pain
    By ten divers plagues, as I shall here declare.

By blood, frogs, and lice; by flies, death, botch and blain;[614]
By hail, by grasshoppers, by darkness, and by care;
By a sudden plague, all their first gotten ware,
Thou slewest, in one night, for his fierce cruelness.
From that thy people withhold not now thy goodness.
PATER CŒLESTIS. I certify thee, my chosen servant Moses,
That people of mine is full of unthankfulness.
MOSES. Dear Lord, I know it, alas! yet weigh their weakness,
And bear with their faults, of thy great bounteousness.
In a flaming bush having to them respect,
Thou appointedst me their passage to direct,
And through the Red Sea thy right hand did us lead
Where Pharaoh's host the flood overwhelmed indeed.
    Thou wentest before them in a shining cloud all day
And in the dark night in fire thou shewedst their way.
Thou sentest them manna from heaven to be their food.
Out of the hard stone thou gavest them water good.
Thou appointedst them a land of milk and honey.
Let them not perish for want of thy great mercy.
PATER CŒLESTIS. Content they are not with foul nor yet with fair,
But murmur and grudge as people in despair.
As I sent manna they had it in disdain,
Thus of their welfare they many times complain.
Over Amalek I gave them the victory.
MOSES. Most glorious Maker, all that is to thy glory.
Thou sentest them also a law from heaven above,
And daily shewedst them many tokens of great love.
The brazen serpent thou gavest them for their healing,
And Balaam's curse thou turnedst into a blessing.
I hope thou wilt not disdain to help them still.
PATER CŒLESTIS. I gave them precepts, which they will not fulfil
Nor yet acknowledge me for their God and good Lord,
So do their vile deeds with their wicked hearts accord
Whilst thou hast talked with me familiarly
On Sinai's mountain, the space but of days forty,
These sights all they have forgotten clearly,
And are turned to shameful idolatry.
For their God, they have set up a golden calf.
MOSES. Let me say something, sweet Father, in their behalf.
PATER CŒLESTIS. I will first conclude, and then say on thy mind.
For that I have found that people so unkind,
Not one of them shall enjoy the promise of me,
For entering the land, but Caleb and Josue.[615]

---

[614] blister.

MOSES. Thy eternal will evermore fulfilled be.

 For disobedience thou slewest the sons of Aaron,

 The earth swallowed in both Dathan and Abiron.

 The adders did sting other wicked persons else,

 In wonderful number. Thus hast thou punished rebels.

PATER CŒLESTIS. Never will I spare the cursed iniquity.

 Of idolatry, for no cause, thou mayst trust me.

MOSES. Forgive them yet, Lord, for this time, if it may be.

PATER CŒLESTIS. Thinkest thou that I will so soon change my decree?

 No, no, friend Moses, so light thou shalt not find me.

 I will punish them all; Israel shall it see.

MOSES. I know, thy people have wrought abomination,

 Worshipping false gods, to thy honour's derogation,

 Yet mercifully thou mayest upon them look;

 And if thou wilt not, thrust me out of thy book.

PATER CŒLESTIS. Those great blasphemers shall out of my book clean,

 But thou shalt not so, for I know what thou dost mean.

 Conduct my people, mine angel shall assist thee,

 That sin in a day will not uncorrected be.

 And for the true zeal that thou to my people hast,

 I add this covenant unto my promises past.

  Raise them up I will a prophet from among them,

 Not unlike to thee, to speak my words unto them.

 Whoso heareth not that he shall speak in my name,

 I will revenge it to his perpetual shame.

 The passover lamb will be a token just

 Of this strong covenant. This have I clearly discussed,

 In my appointment this hour for your deliverance.

MOSES. Never shall this thing depart from my remembrance.

 Praise be for ever to thee, most merciful Lord,

 Who never withdrawest from man thy heavenly comfort,

 But from age to age thy benefits do record

 What thy goodness is, and hath been to his sort.

 As we find thy grace, so ought we to report.

 And doubtless it is to us most bounteous,

 Yea, for all our sins most ripe and plenteous.

  Abraham our father found thee benevolous,[616]

 So did good Isaac in his distress among.

 To Jacob thou wert a guide most gracious.

 Joseph thou savedst from dangerous deadly wrong,

 Melchisedec and Job felt thy great goodness strong,

 So did good Sarah, Rebecca, and fair Rachel,

---

[615] Joshua.

[616] benevolent.

With Zephorah my wife, the daughter of Raguel.
　　To praise thee, sweet Lord, my faith doth me compel,
For thy covenant's sake wherein rests our salvation,
The seed of promise, all other seeds excel,
For therein remaineth our full justification.
From Adam to Noah, in Abraham's generation,
That seed procureth God's mighty grace and power;
For the same seed's sake, I will sing now this hour.

[*Then he begins to sing an antiphon in a clear voice, "O Emmanuel," which the chorus (as before) follows with instruments.*]

O high king Emmanuel, and our liege Lord! the long expectation of the Gentiles, and the mighty Saviour of their multitude, the health and consolation of sinners, come now to save us, as our Lord and our Redeemer.

ACT V

OF PIUS KING DAVID

PATER CŒLESTIS. For all the favour I have shewed Israel,
　　Delivering it from Pharaoh's tyranny,
　　And giving the land, fluentem lac et mel,[617]
　　Yet will it not leave its old idolatry,
　　Nor know me for God. I abhor its misery.
　　Vexed it I have with battles and decays,
　　Still must I plague it, I see no other ways.
DAVID. Remember yet, Lord, thy worthy servant Moses,
　　Walking in thy sight, without rebuke of thee.
　　Both Aaron, Jethro, Eleazar, and Phinees,[618]
　　Evermore feared to offend thy majesty,
　　Much thou acceptedst thy servant Josue.[619]
　　Caleb and Othniel sought thee with all their heart,
　　Aioth and Sangar for thy folk did their part.
　　　Gideon and Tholus thy enemies put to smart,
　　Jair and Jephtha gave praises to thy name.
　　These, to leave idols, thy people did court.
　　Samson the strongest, for his part did the same.
　　Samuel and Nathan thy messages did proclaim.

---

[617] flowing milk and honey.
[618] Phineas.
[619] Joshua.

What though fierce Pharaoh wrought mischief in thy sight,
He was a pagan, lay not that in our light.
    I know the Benjamites abused the ways of right,
So did Eli's sons, and the sons of Samuel.
Saul in his office was slothful day and night,
Wicked was Shimei, so was Ahitophel.
Measure not by them the faults of Israel,
Whom thou hast loved of long time so entirely,
But of thy great grace remit its wicked folly.

PATER CŒLESTIS. I cannot abide the vice of idolatry,
Though I should suffer all other villany.
When Joshua was dead, that sort from me did fall
To the worshipping of Ashteroth and Baal,
Full unclean idols, and monsters bestial.

DAVID. For it they have had thy righteous punishment,
And forasmuch as they did wickedly consent
To the Philistines and Canaanites ungodly
Idolaters, taking to them in matrimony,
Thou threwest them under the King of Mesopotamy,
After thou subduedst them for their idolatry.
    Eighteen years to Eglon, the King of Moabites,
And twenty years to Jabin, the King of Canaanites,
Oppressed they were seven years by the Midianites,
And eighteen years vexed by the cruel Ammonites.
In three great battles, of three score thousand and five,
Of this thy people, not one was left alive.
Have mercy now, Lord, and call them to repentance.

PATER CŒLESTIS. So long as they sin, so long shall they have
    grievance.
David my servant, something must I say to thee,
For that thou lately hast wrought such vanity.

DAVID. Spare not, blessed Lord, but say thy pleasure to me.

PATER CŒLESTIS. Of late days thou hast misused Bathsheba,
The wife of Uriah, and slain him in the field.

DAVID. Mercy, Lord, mercy; for doubtless I am defiled.

PATER CŒLESTIS. I constitute thee a king over Israel,
And thee preserved from Saul, who was thine enemy.
Yea, in my favour, so much thou didst excel,
That of thine enemies I gave thee victory.
Philistines and Syrians to thee came tributary.
Why hast thou then wrought such folly in my sight.
Despising my word, against all godly right?

DAVID. I have sinned, Lord, I beseech thee, pardon me,

PATER CŒLESTIS. Thou shalt not die, David, for this iniquity,
For thy repentance; but thy son by Bathsheba

Shall die, forasmuch as my name is blasphemed
Among my enemies, and thou the worse esteemed.
From thy house for this the sword shall not depart.

DAVID. I am sorry, Lord, from the bottom of my heart.

PATER CŒLESTIS. To further anger thou dost me yet compel.

DAVID. For what matter, Lord? I beseech thy goodness tell.

PATER CŒLESTIS. Why didst thou number the children of Israel?
Supposest in thy mind therein thou hast done well?

DAVID. I cannot say nay, but I have done indiscreetly
To forget thy grace for a human policy.

PATER CŒLESTIS. Thou shalt of these three choose which plague thou
wilt have,
For that sinful act, that I thy soul may save.
A scarceness seven years, or else three months' exile,
If not, for three days a pestilence most vile,
For one thou must have, there is no remedy.

DAVID. Lord, at thy pleasure, for thou art full of mercy.

PATER CŒLESTIS. Of a pestilence then, three score thousand and ten,
In three days shall die of thy most puissant men.

DAVID. O Lord, it is I who have offended thy grace,
Spare them and not me, for I have done the trespace.[620]

PATER CŒLESTIS. Though thy sins be great, thine inward heart's
contribution
Doth move my stomach in wonderful condition.
I find thee a man according to my heart;
Wherefore this promise I make thee, ere I depart.
    A fruit there shall come forth issuing from thy body,
Whom I will advance upon thy seat for ever.
His throne shall become a seat of heavenly glory
His worthy sceptre from right will not dissever,
His happy kingdom, of faith shall perish never.
Of heaven and of earth he was author principal,
And will continue, though they do perish all.
    This sign shalt thou have for a token special,
That thou mayst believe my words unfeignedly,
Where thou hast minded, for my memorial,
To build a temple, thou shalt not finish it truly;
But Solomon thy son shall do that action worthy,
In token that Christ must finish everything
That I have begun, to my praise everlasting.

DAVID. Immortal glory to thee, most heavenly King,
For that thou hast given continual victory
To me thy servant, ever since my annointing,

---

[620] trespass.

And also before, by many conquests worthy.
A bear and lion I slew through thy strength only.
I slew Goliath, who was six cubits long.
Against thine enemies thou madest me ever strong.
  My fleshly frailness made me do deadly wrong,
And clean to forget thy laws of righteousness.
And though thou visitedst my sinfulness among,
With pestilent plagues, and other unquietness;
Yet never tookst thou from me thy plenteousness
Of thy godly spir't, which thou in me didst plant.
I having remorse, thy grace could never want.
  For in conclusion, thy everlasting covenant
Thou gavest unto me for all my wicked sin;
And hast promised here by protestation constant,
That one of my seed shall such high fortune win,
As never did man since this world did begin.
By his power he shall put Satan from his hold,
In rejoice whereof to sing will I be bold.

[*Then he begins in a musical voice an antiphon, "O Adonai,"
which the chorus (as before) follows with instruments.*]

O Lord God Adonai, and guide of the faithful house of Israel,
who sometime appearedst in the flaming bush to Moses, and to
him didst give a law on Mount Sinai, come now to redeem us in
the strength of thy right hand.

ACT VI

OF THE PROPHET ESAIAS

PATER CŒLESTIS. I brought up children from their first infancy,
    Who now despise all my godly instructions.
    An ox knoweth its lord, an ass its master's duty,
    But Israel will not know me, nor my conditions.
    Oh, froward people, given all to superstitions,
    Unnatural children, expert in blasphemies,
    Provoke me into hate, by their idolatries.
      Take heed to my words, ye tyrants of Sodoma,
    In vain ye offer your sacrifice to me.
    Discontent I am with you beasts of Gomorrah
    And have no pleasure when I your offerings see.
    I abhor your fasts and your solemnity,
    For your traditions my ways ye set apart,
    Your works are in vain, I hate them from the heart.

ESAIAS. Thy city, sweet Lord, is now become unfaithful,
    And her conditions are turned upside down.
    Her life is unchaste, her acts be very hurtful,
    Her murder and theft have darkened her renown.
    Covetous rewards do so their conscience drown,
    That the fatherless they will not help to right,
    The poor widow's cause comes not before their sight.
       Thy peaceable paths seek they neither day nor night;
    But walk wicked ways after their fantasy.
    Convert their hearts, Lord, and give them thy true light,
    That they may perceive their customable folly:
    Leave them not helpless in so deep misery,
    But call them from it of thy most special grace,
    By thy true prophets, to their souls' health and solace.
PATER CŒLESTIS. First they had fathers, then had they patriarchs,
    Then dukes, then judges for their guides and monarchs:
    Now have they stout kings, yet are they wicked still,
    And will in no wise my pleasant laws fulfil.
    Always they apply to idols' worshipping,
    From the vile beggar to the annointed king.
ESAIAS. For that cause thou hast in two divided them,
    In Samaria the one, the other in Jerusalem.
    The king of Judah in Jerusalem did dwell,
    And in Samaria the king of Israel.
    Ten of the twelve tribes became Samaritans,
    And the other two were Hierosolymitans.[621]
       In both these countries, according to their doings,
    Thou permittedst them to have most cruel kings.
    The first of Judah was wicked king Roboam,
    Of Israel the first was that cruel Jeroboam;
    Abiah then followed, and in the other Nadab,
    Then Bassa, then Helah, then Zambri, Jehoram and Ahab.
       Then Ochesius, then Athaliah, then Joas;[622]
    On the other part was Jonathan and Achaz.
    To rehearse all them that have done wretchedly
    In the sight of thee, it were long verily.
PATER CŒLESTIS. For the wicked sin of filthy idolatry,
    Which the ten tribes did in the land of Samarie,
    In space of one day fifty thousand men I slew,
    Three of their cities also I overthrew,
    And left the people in such captivity,
    That in all the world they knew not whither to flee.

---

[621] inhabitants of Jerusalem.
[622] Joash.

The other two tribes, when they from me went back
To idolatry, I left in the hand of Shishak,
The king of Egypt, who took away their treasure,
Conveyed their cattle, and slew them without measure.
In time of Ahaz, a hundred thousand and twenty
Were slain at one time for their idolatry.
    Two hundred thousand from thence were captive led,
Their goods dispersed, and they with penury fed.
Seldom they fail it, but either the Egyptians
Have them in bondage, or else the Assyrians.

ESAIAS. Well, yet blessed Lord, relieve them with thy mercy.
Though they have been ill other princes' days,
Yet good Hezekiah hath taught them goodly ways.
When the prince is good, the people are the better;
And as he is nought, their vices are the greater.
Heavenly Lord, therefore send them the consolation,
Which thou hast covenanted with every generation.
    Open thou the heavens, and let the lamb come hither,
Who will deliver thy people altogether.
Ye planets and clouds, cast down your dews and rain,
That the earth may bear out healthful savour plain.

PATER CŒLESTIS. May the wife forget the child of her own body?

ESAIAS. Nay, that she can not in any wise verily.

PATER CŒLESTIS. No more can I them who will do my commandments,
But must preserve them from all inconvenience.

ESAIAS. Blessed art thou, Lord, in all thy acts and judgments.

PATER CŒLESTIS. Well, Esaias, for this thy fidelity,
A covenant of health thou shalt have also of me.
For Zion's sake now I will not hold my peace,
And for Jerusalem, to speak will I not cease
Till that righteous Lord become as a sunbeam bright,
And their just saviour as a lamp extend his light.
    A rod shall shoot forth from the old stock of Jesse,
And a bright blossom from that root will arise,
Upon whom always the spir't of the Lord shall be,
The spir't of wisdom, the spir't of heavenly practice,
And the spir't that will all godliness devise.
Take this for a sign, a maid of Israel
Shall conceive and bear that Lord Emmanuel.

ESAIAS. Thy praises condign no mortal tongue can tell,
Most worthy maker and king of heavenly glory,
For all capacities thy goodness doth excel,
Thy plenteous graces no brain can compass truly,
No wit can conceive the greatness of thy mercy,
Declared of late in David thy true servant,

And now confirmed in this thy later covenant.
    Of goodness thou madest Solomon of wit more pregnant,
Asa and Josaphat, with good king Hezechiah,
In thy sight to do that was to thee right pleasant.
To quench idolatry thou raisedst up Elijah
Jehu, Elisha, Micah, and Obdiah,
The Syrian Naaman thou purgedst of a lepry[623]
Thy works wonderful who can but magnify?
    Arise, Jerusalem, and take faith by and by,[624]
For the very light that shall save thee is coming.
The Son of the Lord appear will evidently,
When he shall resort, see that no joy be wanting.
He is thy saviour, and thy life everlasting,
Thy release from sin, and thy whole righteousness,
Help me in this song t' acknowledge his great goodness.

[*Then in a tuneful voice he begins an antiphon, "O radix Jesse,"
which the chorus follows with instruments.*]

O fruitful root of Jesse, that shall be set as a sign among people, against the worldly rulers shall fiercely open their mouths, whom the Gentiles worship as their heavenly Lord. Come now to deliver us, and delay the time no longer.

ACT VII

OF JOHN THE BAPTIST

PATER CŒLESTIS. I have with fierceness mankind oft-times corrected,
    And again I have allured him by sweet promise.
I have sent sore plagues, when he hath me neglected,
And then by and by, most comfortable sweetness.
To win him to grace, both mercy and righteousness
I have exercised, yet will he not amend.
Shall I now lose him, or shall I him defend?
    In his most mischief, most high grace will I send
To overcome him by favour, if it may be.
With his abuses no longer will I contend
But now accomplish my first will and decree.
My word being flesh, from hence shall set him free,
Him teaching a way of perfect righteousness,
That he shall not need to perish in his weakness.

---

[623] leprosy.
[624] immediately.

JOHN THE BAPTIST. Manasseh is past, who turned from thee his heart.
Ahaz and Ammon have now no more ado,
Jechoniah with others who did themselves avert
From thee to idols, may now no farther go.
The two false judges, and Baal's wicked priests also,
Phassur and Semaiah, with Nebuchadnosor,
Antiochus and Triphon, shall thee displease no more.
Three score years and ten, thy people into Babylon
Were captive and thrall for idols' worshipping.
Jerusalem was lost, and left void of dominion,
Burnt was their temple, so was their other building,
Their high priests were slain, their treasure came to nothing;
The strength and beauty of thine own heritage,
Thus didst thou leave them in miserable bondage.
Oft had they warnings, sometimes by Ezekiel
And other prophets, as Isay and Jeremy,
Sometimes by Daniel, sometimes by Hosea and Joel,
By Amos and Abdiah, by Jonah and Sophonya,[625]
By Nahum and Micah, Haggai and by Zachary,
By Malachias, and also by Habakkuk,
By Olda the widow, and by the prophet Baruch.
Remember Josiah, who took the abomination
From the people, then restoring the laws again.
Of Rahab consider the faithful generation,
Whom to wine drinking no friendship might constrain.
Remember Abimelech, the friend of truth certain,
Zerubabel the prince, who did repair the temple,
And Jesus Josedech, of virtue the example.
Consider Nehemiah, and Esdras the good scribe,
Merciful Tobias, and constant Mardocheus;[626]
Judith and Queen Esther, of the same godly tribe,
Devout Matthias and Judas Maccabæus.
Have mind of Eleazer, and then Joannes Hircanus,
Weigh the earnest faith of this godly company,
Though the other clean fall from thy memory.
PATER CŒLESTIS. I will John, I will, for as I said before,
Rigour and hardness I have now set apart,
Minding from henceforth to win man evermore
By wonderful kindness to break his stubborn heart,
And change it from sin. For Christ shall suffer smart,
In man's frail nature for his iniquity,
This to make open, my messenger shalt thou be.

---

[625] Zephaniah
[626] Mordecai.

JOHN THE BAPTIST. As thy pleasure is, so blessed Lord appoint me,
    For my health thou art, and my soul's felicity.
PATER CŒLESTIS. Long ere I made thee, I the predestinate,
    Before thou wert born I thee endued with grace.
    In thy mother's womb wert thou sanctificate
    By my godly gift, and so confirmed in place,
    A prophet, to shew a way before the face
    Of my most dear son, who will come: then until
    Apply thee apace thine office to fulfil.
      Preach to the people, rebuking their negligence,
    Dip them in water, acknowledging their offence;
    And say unto them, The kingdom of God doth come.
JOHN THE BAPTIST. Unmeet, Lord, I am, Quia puer ego sum.[627]
    And other than that, alas, I have no science
    Fit for that office, neither yet clean eloquence.
PATER CŒLESTIS. Thou shalt not say so, for I have given thee grace,
    Eloquence and age, to speak in desert place.
    Thou must do therefore as I shall thee advise,
    My appointed pleasure forth utter in any wise;
    My strong mighty words put I into thy mouth,
    Spare not, but speak them to east, west, north and south.

    [GOD *stretching out his hand, touches* JOHN'S *lips with his finger
    and confers upon him a golden tongue.*]

    Go now thy way forth, I shall thee never fail,
    The spir't of Elijah have I given thee already.
    Persuade the people, that they their sins bewail;
    And if they repent their customable folly,
    Long shall it not be ere they have remedy.
    Open thou their hearts: tell them their health is coming
    As a voice in a desert; see thou declare the thing.
      I promise thee sure, thou shalt wash him among them
    In Jordan, a flood not far from Jerusalem.
JOHN THE BAPTIST. Shew me yet, good Lord, whereby shall I know that
      man,
    In the multitude which will resort to Jordan.
PATER CŒLESTIS. In thy mother's womb of him hadst thou cognition.
    Have thou no fear John, him shalt thou know full well,
    And one special token afore will I thee tell.
    Super quem videris spiritum descendentem et manentem
    Super eum, hic est qui baptizat spiritu sancto:
    Among all other whom thou shalt baptise there

---

[627] Because I am a youth.

Upon whom thou seest the Holy Ghost descend
In shape of a dove, resting upon his shoulder,
Hold him for the same, that shall the world amend,
By baptism of spirit, and also to man extend
Most special grace. For he must repair his fall,
Restoring again the justice original.
Take now thy journey, and do as I thee advise,
First preach repentance, and then the people baptise.
JOHN THE BAPTIST. High honour, worship, and glory be unto thee,
My God eternal, and patron of all purity.
 Repent good people, for sins that now are past,
The kingdom of heaven is at hand very nigh.
The promised light to you approacheth fast,
Have faith, and apply now to receive him boldly.
I am not the light, but to bear testimony
Of him am sent, that all men may believe,
That his blood he will for their redemption give.
 He is such a light as all men doth illumine,
That ever were here, or shall be after this.
All the world he made by his mighty power divine,
And yet that rude world will not know what he is.
His own he entering, is not regarded of his.
They that receive him, are God's true children plain,
In spir't regenerate, and all grace shall attain.
 Many do reckon, that I John Baptist am he,
Deceived are they, and that will appear in space.
Though he come after, yet he was long afore me.
We are weak vessels, he is the well of grace,
Of his great goodness all that we have we purchase.
By him are we like to have a better increase
Than ever we had by the laws of Moses.
 For Moses' hard law we had not else but darkness,
Figure and shadow, all was not else but night,
Punishment for sin, much rigour, pain, and roughness,
An high charge is there, where all is turned to light,
Grace and remission anon will shine full bright.
Never man lived that ever saw God afore,
Which now in our kind man's ruin will restore.
 Help me to give thanks to that Lord evermore,
Which am unto Christ a crier in the desert,
To prepare the paths and high ways him before
For his delight is on the poor, simple heart.
 That innocent lamb from such will never depart,
As will faithfully receive him with good mind.
Let our voice then sound in some sweet musical kind.

[*Then in a resounding voice he begins an antiphon, "O clavis
David," which the chorus follows with instruments, as before.*]

O perfect key of David, and high sceptre of the kindred of
Jacob, which openest and no man sperith,[628] thou speakest and no
man openeth; come and deliver thy servant mankind, bound in
prison, sitting in the darkness of sin and bitter damnation.

EPILOGUE

BALEUS PROLOCUTOR. The matters are such as we have uttered here,
    As ought not to slide from your memorial;
    For they have opened such comfortable gear,
    As is to the health of this kind universal,
    Graces of the Lord and promises liberal,
    Which he given to man for every age,
    To knit him to Christ, and so clear him of bondage.
    As St. Paul doth write unto the Corinthes[629] plain,
    Our forefathers were under the cloud of darkness,
    And unto Christ's days did in the shadow remain;
    Yet were they not left, for of him they had promise
    All they received one spiritual feeding doubtless.
    They drank of the rock which them to life refreshed,
    For one saving health, in Christ, all they confessed.
    In the woman's seed was Adam first justified,
    So was faithful Noah, so was just Abraham;
    The faith in that seed in Moses forth multiplied,
    Likewise in David and Esaye[630] that after came,
    And in John Baptist, which shewed the very Lamb.
    Though they so afar, yet all they had one justice
    One mass, as they call it, and in Christ one sacrifice.
    A man cannot here to God do better service,
    Than on this to ground his faith and understanding.
    For all the world's sin alone Christ payed the price,
    In his only death was man's life always resting,
    And not in will—works, nor yet in men's deserving,
    The light of our faith makes this thing evident,
    And not the practice of other experiment.
    Where is now free will, which the hypocrites comment?
    Whereby they report they may at their own pleasure

---

[628] asks.
[629] Corinthians.
[630] Esaias.

Do good of themselves, though grace and faith be absent,
And have good intents their madness with to measure.
The will of the flesh is proved here small treasure,
And so is man's will, for the grace of God doth all.
More of this matter conclude hereafter we shall.

Thus endeth this tragedy or interlude, manifesting the chief promises of God unto Man by all ages in the old law, from the fall of Adam to the incarnation of the Lord Jesus Christ. Compiled by John Bayle. Anno Domini 1538.

Appendices

APPENDIX A

"ST. GEORGE AND THE DRAGON"

A MODERN CORNISH CHRISTMAS PLAY

CHARACTERS

SAINT GEORGE
THE DRAGON
FATHER CHRISTMAS
THE DOCTOR
KING OF EGYPT
TURKISH KNIGHT
THE GIANT TURPIN

[*Enter the* TURKISH KNIGHT.]

Open your doors, and let me in,
I hope your favours I shall win;
Whether I rise or whether I fall,
I'll do my best to please you all.
St. George is here, and swears he will come in,
And, if he does, I know he'll pierce my skin.
If you will not believe what I do say,
Let Father Christmas come in—clear the way. [*Retires.*]

[*Enter* FATHER CHRISTMAS.]

Here come I, old Father Christmas,
     Welcome, or welcome not,
I hope old Father Christmas
     Will never be forgot.

I am not come here to laugh or to jeer,
But for a pocketfull of money, and a skinfull of beer,
If you will not believe what I do say,
Come in, the King of Egypt!—clear the way!

[*Enter the* KING OF EGYPT.]

Here I, the King of Egypt, boldly do appear,
St. George, St. George, walk in, my only son and heir.
Walk in, my son St. George, and boldly act thy part,
That all the people here may see thy wond'rous art.

[*Enter* SAINT GEORGE.]

Here come I, St. George, from Britain did I spring,
I'll fight the Dragon bold, my wonders to begin.
I'll clip his wings, he shall not fly;
I'll cut him down, or else I die.

[*Enter the* DRAGON.]

Who's he that seeks the Dragon's blood,
And calls so angry, and so loud?
That English dog, will he before me stand?
I'll cut him down with my courageous hand.
With my long teeth, and scurvy jaw,
Of such I'd break up half a score,
And stay my stomach, till I'd more.

[ST. GEORGE *and the* DRAGON *fight, the latter is killed.*]

FATHER CHRISTMAS. Is there a doctor to be found
        All ready, near at hand,
To cure a deep and deadly wound,
        And make the champion stand.

[*Enter* DOCTOR.]

Oh! yes, there is a doctor to be found
        All ready, near at hand,
To cure a deep and deadly wound,
        And make the champion stand.
FATHER CHRISTMAS. What can you cure?
DOCTOR. All sorts of diseases,
    Whatever you pleases,
    The phthisic, the palsy, and the gout;
    If the devil's in, I'll blow him out.
FATHER CHRISTMAS. What is your fee?
DOCTOR. Fifteen pound, it is my fee,
        The money to lay down.
    But, as 'tis such a rogue as thee,

I cure for ten pound.

I carry a little bottle of alicumpane;
        Here Jack, take a little of my flip flop,
        Pour it down thy tip top;
Rise up and fight again.

[*The* DOCTOR *performs his cure, the fight is renewed, and the* DRAGON *again killed.*]

SAINT GEORGE. Here am I, St. George,
        That worthy champion bold,
And with my sword and spear
        I won three crowns of gold.
I fought the fiery dragon,
        And brought him to the slaughter;
By that I won fair Sabra,
        The King of Egypt's daughter.
Where is the man, that now will me defy?
I'll cut his giblets full of holes, and make his buttons fly.

[*The* TURKISH KNIGHT *advances.*]

Here come I, the Turkish Knight,
Come from the Turkish land to fight.
I'll fight St. George, who is my foe,
I'll make him yield before I go;
He brags to such a high degree,
He thinks there's none can do the like of he.
SAINT GEORGE. Where is the Turk, that will before me stand?
        I'll cut him down with my courageous hand.

[*They fight, the* KNIGHT *is overcome, and falls on one knee.*]

Turkish Knight. Oh! pardon me, St. George, pardon of thee I crave,
        Oh! pardon me this night, and I will be thy slave.
SAINT GEORGE. No pardon shalt thou have, while I have foot to stand,
        So rise thee up again, and fight out sword in hand.

[*They fight again, and the* KNIGHT *is killed.* FATHER CHRISTMAS *calls for the* DOCTOR, *with whom the same dialogue occurs as before, and the cure is performed.*]

[*Enter the* GIANT TURPIN.]

Here come I, the Giant, bold Turpin is my name,
And all the nations round do tremble at my fame.
Where'er I go, they tremble at my sight,
No lord or champion long with me would fight.
SAINT GEORGE. Here's one that dares to look thee in the face,
And soon will send thee to another place.

[*They fight, and the* GIANT *is killed; medical aid is called in as
before, and the cure performed by the* DOCTOR, *to whom then
is given a basin of girdy grout and a kick, and driven out.*]

FATHER CHRISTMAS. Now, ladies and gentlemen, your sport is most
ended,
So prepare for the hat, which is highly commended.
The hat it would speak, if it had but a tongue;
Come throw in your money, and think it no wrong.

APPENDIX B

FROM THE CORNISH MYSTERY OF THE CRUCIFIXION

JESUS. Woman, seest thou thy son?
A thousand times your arms have borne him
With tenderness.
And John, behold thy mother;
Thus keep her, without denial,
As long as ye live.
MARY. Alas! alas! oh! sad, sad!
In my heart is sorrow,
When I see my son Jesus,
About his head a crown of thorns
He is Son of God in every way,
And with that truly a King;
Feet and hands on every side
Fast fixed with nails of iron.
Alas!
That one shall have on the day of judgment
Heavy doom, flesh and blood,
Who hath sold him.
JOHN. O sweet mother, do not bear sorrow,
For always, in every way
I will be prepared for thee:
The will of thy Son is so,
For to save so much as is good,
Since Adam was created.

JESUS. O Father, Eli, Eloy, · lama sabacthani?
    Thou art my dear God,
    Why hast thou left me · a moment alone
    In any manner?
1ST EXECUTIONER. He is calling Elias;
    Watch now diligently
      If he comes to save him.
    If he delivers him, really
    We will believe in him,
      And worship him ever.

[*Here a sponge is made ready, with gall and vinegar. And then the
    Centurion stands in his tent, and says:*]

CENTURION. I will go to see
    How it is with dear Jesus:
    It were a pity on a good man
      So much contumely to be cast.
    If he were a bad man, his fellow
      Could not in any way
    Truly have such great grace,
      To save men by one word.

[*The* CENTURION *goes down.*]

2ND EXECUTIONER. It is not Elias whom he called;
    Thirst surely on him there is,
      He finds it an evil thing. [*He holds out a sponge.*]
    Behold here I have me ready,
    Gall and hyssop mixed;
      Wassail, if there is great thirst.
JESUS. Thirst on me there is.
3RD EXECUTIONER. See, a drink for thee here;
    Why dost thou not drink it?
    Rather shouldst thou a wonder work!
    Now, come down from the cross,
      And we will worship thee.
JESUS. O Father, into thy hands
    I commit my spirit;
    By thy will take it to thee,
    As thou sent it into the world.

[*Then* JESUS *shall die. Here the sun is darkened.*]

THE TOWN CYCLES

I.—THE YORK PAGEANTS

The order of the Pageants of the Play of Corpus Christi, in the time of the mayoralty of William Alne, in the third year of the reign of King Henry V. anno 1415, compiled by Roger Burton, town clerk,—

I. Tanners.—God the Father Almighty creating and forming the heavens, angels and archangels; Lucifer and the angels that fell with him into hell.

II. Plasterers.—God the Father, in his own substance, creating the earth, and all which is therein, in the space of five days.

III. Carde-makers.—God the Father creating Adam of the slime of the earth, and making Eve of the rib, and inspiring them with the spirit of life.

IV. Fullers.—God prohibiting Adam and Eve from eating of the tree of life.

V. Coupers.—Adam and Eve with a tree betwixt them; the serpent deceiving them with apples; God speaking to them and cursing the serpent, and an angel with a sword driving them out of paradise.

VI. Armourers.—Adam and Eve, an angel with a spade and a distaff assigning them labour.

VII. Gaunters.—Abel and Cain killing sacrifices.

VIII. Shipwrights.—God foretelling Noah to make an ark of light wood.

IX. Fyshmongers, Pessyners, Mariners.—Noah in the ark with his wife and three children, and divers animals.

X. Perchemyners, Bukbynders.—Abraham sacrificing his son Isaac; a ram, bush, and angel.

XI. Hosyers.—Moses exalting the serpent in the wilderness; king Pharaoh; eight Jews admiring and expecting.

XII. Spicers.—Mary and a doctor declaring the sayings of the prophets about the future birth of Christ; an angel saluting her. Mary saluting Elizabeth.

XIII. Peuterers, Founders.—Mary, Joseph willing to put her away, an angel speaking to them that they should go to Bethlehem.

XIV. Tylers.—Mary, Joseph, a midwife, the child born lying in a manger betwixt an ox and an ass, and the angel speaking to the shepherds.

XV. Chaundelers.—The shepherds speaking by turns; the star in the east; an angel giving joy to the shepherds that a child was born.

XVI. Goldsmithes, Orfeures.—The three kings coming from the

east, Herod asking them about the child Christ; with the son of Herod, two counsellors and a messenger.

XVII. Gold-beters, Mone-makers.—Mary with the child and the star above, and the three kings offering gifts.

XVIII. Masons.—Mary with the child; Joseph, Anna, and a nurse with young pigeons; Simeon receiving the child in his arms, and two sons of Simeon.

XIX. Marashals.—Mary with the child, and Joseph flying into Egypt, by an angel's telling them.

XX. Girdellers, Naylers, Sawters.—Herod commanding the children to be slain, four soldiers with lances, two counsellors of the king, and four women lamenting the slaughter of them.

XXI. Sporiers, Lorymers.—The doctors, the child Jesus sitting in the temple in the midst of them, hearing them and asking them questions. Four Jews, Mary and Joseph seeking him and finding him in the temple.

XXII. Barbers.—Jesus, John the baptist baptising him, and two angels helping them.

XXIII. Vyntners.—Jesus, Mary, bridgeroom and bride, master of the household with his family with six water-pots, where water is turned into wine.

XXIV. Smythes, Fevers.—Jesus upon the pinnacle of the temple; Satan tempting with stones; two angels administering, etc.

XXV. C [orvisors.] —Peter, James and John; Jesus ascending into the mountain and transfiguring himself before them. Moses and Elias appearing, and a voice speaking from a cloud.

XXVI. Elennagers.—Simon the leper asking Jesus if he would eat with him. Two disciples; Mary Magdalene washing the feet of Jesus, and wiping them with her hair.

XXVII. Plummers, Patten-makers.—Jesus, two Apostles, the woman taken in adultery, four Jews accusing her.

XXVIII. Pouch-makers, Botillers, Cap-makers.—Lazarus in the sepurchre; Mary Magdalene, Martha, and two Jews admiring.

XXIX. Vestment-makers, Skynners.—Jesus upon an ass with its foal; twelve Apostles following Jesus; six rich and six poor men, with eight boys with branches of palm trees, constantly saying blessed, etc., and Zaccheus ascending into a sycamore tree.

XXX. Cuttelers, Blade-smythes, Shethers, Scalers, Buklemakers, Horners.—Pilate, Caiaphas, two soldiers, three Jews, Judas selling Jesus.

XXXI. Bakers, Waterleders.—The supper of the Lord and paschal Lamb, twelve apostles; Jesus, tied about with a linen towel, washing their feet. The institution of the sacrament of the body of Christ in the new law, and communion of the Apostles.

XXXII. Cordwaners.—Pilate, Caiaphas, Annas, forty armed

soldiers, Malchas, Peter, James, John, Jesus, and Judas kissing and betraying him.

XXXIII. Bowers, Fletchers.—Jesus, Annas, Caiaphas, and four Jews striking and bastinadoing Christ. Peter, the woman accusing him, and Malchas.

XXXIV. Tapisers, Couchers.—Jesus, Pilate, Annas, Caiaphas; two counsellors and four Jews accusing Christ.

XXXV. Littesters.—Herod, two counsellors, four soldiers, Jesus, and three Jews.

XXXVI. Cukes, Water-leders.—Pilate, Annas, Caiaphas, two Jews, and Judas carrying from them thirty pieces of silver.

XXXVII. Sauce-makers.—Judas hanging himself.

XXXVIII. Milners, Tiel-makers, Ropers, Cevers, Turners, Hayresters, Bollers.—Jesus, Pilate, Caiaphas, Annas, six soldiers carrying spears and ensigns, and other four leading Jesus from Herod desiring Barabbas to be released and Jesus to be crucified, and then binding and scourging him, putting a crown of thorns upon his head; three soldiers casting lots for the vesture of Jesus.

XXXIX. Shermen.—Jesus covered with blood bearing his cross towards mount Calvary, Simon Sereneus, etc.

XL. Pynners, Lateners, Paynters.—The cross, Jesus extended upon it on the earth; four Jews scourging him with whips, and afterwards erecting the cross, with Jesus upon it, on Mount Calvary.

XLI. Bouchers, Pulterers.—The cross, two thieves crucified and Jesus suspended betwixt them; Mary the mother of Jesus, John, Mary, James and Salome; a soldier with a lance, and a servant with a sponge. Pilate, Annas, Caiaphas, a centurion, Joseph of Arimathea, and Nicodemus taking him down and laying him in the sepulchre.

XLII. Satellers, Sellers, Glasiers.—Jesus destroying hell; twelve good and twelve evil spirits.

XLIII. Carpenters, Joyners.—The centurion declaring to Pilate, Caiaphas and Annas, with other Jews, the signs appearing on the death of Jesus.

XLIV. Cartwrights, Carvers, Sawyers.—Jesus rising from the sepulchre, four soldiers armed, and three Marias lamenting; Pilate, Caiaphas, and Annas; a young man clothed in white sitting in the sepulchre and talking to the women.

XLV. Wyedrawers.—Jesus, Mary, Mary Magdalene with spices.

XLVI. Broggers, Wool-pakkers, Wadsmen.—Jesus, Luke and Cleophas in the form of travellers.

XLVII. Escriviners, Lumners, Questors, Dubbors.—Jesus, Peter, John, James, Philip and other Apostles; Thomas feeling the wounds of Jesus.

XLVIII. Taillyoures.—Mary, John the Evangelist, two angels, and eleven Apostles; Jesus ascending before them, and four angels bearing a cloud.

XLIX. Potters.—Mary, two angels, eleven Apostles, the Holy Ghost descending upon them, and four Jews admiring.

L. Drapers.—Jesus, Mary, Gabriel with two angels, two virgins and three Jews of the kindred of Mary, eight Apostles, and two devils.

LI. Lynwevers.—Four Apostles bearing the shrine of Mary, Fergus hanging upon it with two other Jews, and one angel.

LII. Wevers of wollen.—Mary ascending with a multitude of angels; eight Apostles, with Thomas preaching in the desert.

LIII. Hostilers.—Mary, and Jesus crowning her with a great number of angels.

LIV. Mercers.—Jesus, Mary, twelve Apostles; four angels with trumpets, and four with a lance with two scourges; four good and four bad spirits, and six devils.

II.—THE WAKEFIELD (OR WOODKIRK) PLAYS

From the Towneley Collection

I. Creatio. II. Mactatio Abel. III. Processus Noe cum filiis. IV. Abraham. V. Isaac. VI. Jacob. VII. Processus Prophetarum. VIII. Pharao. IX. Cæsar Augustus. X. Annunciatio. XI. Salutatio Elizabeth. XII. Prima Pagina Pastorum. XIII. Secunda Pagina Pastorum. XIV. Oblatio Magorum. XV. Fugatio Joseph et Mariæ in Egyptum. XVI. Magnus Herodes. XVII. Purificatio Mariæ. XVIII. Pagina Doctorum. XIX. Johannes Baptista. XX. Conspiratio et Captio. XXI. Coliphizatio. XXII. Flagellatio. XXIII. Processus Crucis. XXIV. Processus Talentorum. XXV. Extractio Animarum ab Inferno. XXVI. Resurrectio Domini. XXVII. Peregrini. XXVIII. Thomas Indiæ. XXIX. Ascensio Domini. XXX. Juditium. XXXI. Lazarus. XXXII. Suspensio Judæ.

III.—THE CHESTER PLAYS

I. The Fall of Lucifer, by the Tanners.

II. The Creation, by the Drapers.

III. The Deluge, by the Dyers.

IV. Abraham, Melchisedech, and Lot, by the Barbers and Wax-chandlers.

V. Moses, Balak, and Balaam, by the Hatters and Linen-drapers.

VI. The Salutation and Nativity, by the Wrights.

VII. The Shepherds feeding their flocks by night, by the Painters and Glaziers.

VIII. The three Kings, by the Vintners.

IX. The Oblation of the three Kings, by the Mercers.

X. The Killing of the Innocents, by the Goldsmiths.

XI. The Purification, by the Blacksmiths.

XII. The Temptation, by the Butchers.

XIII. The Blindmen and Lazarus, by the Glovers.

XIV. Jesus and the Lepers, by the Corvisors.

XV. The last Supper, by the Bakers.

XVI. The Passion and Crucifixion of Christ, by the Fletchers, Coopers, and Ironmongers.

XVII. The Descent into Hell, by the Cooks.

XVIII. The Resurrection, by the Skinners.

XIX. The Appearing of Christ to the two Disciples, by the Saddlers.

XX. The Ascension, by the Tailors.

XXI. The Election of St. Mathias, sending of the Holy Ghost, by the Fishmongers.

XXII. Ezekiel, by the Clothiers.

XXIII. Antichrist, by the Dyers.

XXIV. The Day of Judgement, by the Websters.

IV—THE LUDUS COVENTRIÆ[631]

I. The Creation. II. The Fall of Man. III. The Death of Abel. IV. Noah's Flood. V. Abraham's Sacrifice. VI. Moses and the Two Tables. VII. The Genealogy of Christ. VIII. Anna's Pregnancy. IX. Mary in the Temple. X. Her Betrothment. XI. The Salutation and Conception. XII. Joseph's Return. XIII. The Visit to Elizabeth. XIV. The Trial of Joseph and Mary. XV. The Birth of Christ. XVI. The Shepherd's Offering. XVII. Caret in MS. XVIII. Adoration of the Magi. XIX. The Purification. XX. Slaughter of the Innocents. XXI. Christ disputing in the Temple. XXII. The Baptism of Christ. XXIII. The Temptation. XXIV. The Woman taken in Adultery. XXV. Lazarus. XXVI. Council of the Jews. XXVII. Mary Magdalen. XXVIII. Christ betrayed. XXIX. Herod. XXX. The Trial of Christ. XXXI. The Dream of Pilate's Wife. XXXII. The Crucifixion. XXXIII. The Descent into Hell. XXXIV. Sealing of the Tomb. XXXV. The Resurrection. XXXVI. The Three Marias. XXXVII. Christ appearing to Mary Magdalen. XXXVIII. The Pilgrim of Emaus. XXXIX. The Ascension. XL. Descent of the Holy Ghost. XLI. The Assumption of the Virgin. XLII. Doomsday.

---

[631] Though this is called the Ludus Coventriæ, there is no evidence that the cycle ever was played at Coventry, or that at any time more than ten pageants were produced there by the town guilds. The Coventry Nativity Play that we print (from the text of Robert Croo, 1534) is one of the ten] It was played by the "Company of Shearmen and Tailors."

APPENDIX D

I.—Properties and Dresses used for the Coventry Smiths' Pageant of the Trial, Condemnation, and Crucifixion of Christ between the Years 1449 and 1585

> The Cross with a Rope to draw it up, and a Curtain hanging before it.
> Gilding for the Pillar and the Cross.
> 2 Pair of Gallows.
> 4 Scourges and a Pillar.
> Scaffold.
> Fanes to the Pageant.
> Mending of Imagery occurs 1469.
> A Standard of red Buckram.
> Two red Pensiles of Cloth painted, and silk Fringe.
> Iron to hold up the Streamer.
> 4 Gowns and 4 Hoods for the Tormentors.—(These are afterwards described as Jackets of black buckram with nails and dice upon them.) Other 4 gowns with damask flowers; also 2 Jackets party red and black.
> 2 Mitres (for Cayphas and Annas).
> A Rochet for one of the Bishops.
> God's Coat of white leather, 6 skins.
> A Staff for the Demon.
> 2 Spears.
> Gloves (12 pair at once).
> Herod's Crest of Iron.
> Scarlet Hoods and a Tabard.
> Hats and Caps.
> Cheverel [Peruke] for God.
> 3 Cheverels and a Beard.
> 2 Cheverels gilt for Jesus and Peter.
> Faulchion for Herod.
> Scarlet Gown.
> Maces.

II.—The Chester "Bannes" or Bans

Reverende lordes and ladyes all,
That at this time here assembled bee,
By this messuage understande you shall,
That sometymes there was mayor of this citie,
Sir John Arnway, Knyghte, who most worthilye
Contented himselfe to set out an playe
The devise of one Done Randali, moonke of Chester Abbey.

"This moonke, moonke-like, in scriptures well seene,
In storyes travelled with the best sorte;
In pagentes set fourth, apparently to all eyne,
The Olde and Newe Testament with livelye comforte;
Intermynglinge therewith, onely to make sporte,
Some things not warranted by any writt,
Which to gladd the hearers he woulde men to take yt.

"This matter he abrevited into playes twenty-foure,
And every playe of the matter gave but a taste,
Leavinge for better learninges circumstances to accomplishe,
For his proceedinges maye appeare to be in haste:
Yet all together unprofitable his labour he did not waste,
For at this daye, and ever, he deserveth the fame
Which all moonkes deserve professinge that name.

"This worthy Knyghte Arnway, then mayor of this citie,
This order toke, as declare to you I shall,
That by twenty-fower occupations, artes, craftes, or misteries,
These pagentes shoulde be played affter breeffe rehearsall;
For every pagente a cariage to be provyded withall,
In which sorte we purpose this Whitsontyde,
Our pagentes into three partes to devyde.

"Now you worshippful Tanners that of custume olde
The fall of Lucifer did set out,
Some writers awarrante your matter, therefore be boulde
Lustelye to playe the same to all the rowtte;
And yf any thereof stand in any doubte,
Your author his author hath, your shewe let bee,
Good speech, fyne players, with apparill comelye.

"The good symple water-leaders and drawers of deey,
See that your Arke in all poyntes be prepared;

Of Noy and his children the wholl storye,
And of the universall floude, by you shalbe played.

"The Sacrifice that faithfull Abraham of his sonne should make,
You barbers and waxe-chaundlers of Aunciente tyme,
In the fourth pageante with paines you doe take,
In decente sorte set out—the storie is ffine—
The offeringe of Melchesedecke of breade and wine,
And the presentacion therof set in your playe,
Suffer you not in any poynte the story to decaye.

III.—Cornish Miracle Plays

[From Norris's "Ancient Cornish Drama"]

We have no notice of the performance of the Cornish plays earlier than that of Richard Carew, whose survey of Cornwall was first printed in 1602. In his time they even played in regular amphitheatres, and the account he gives is well worth extracting, as it affords a vivid picture by one who was in all probability an eye-witness, nearly three centuries ago. "The quasy miracle, in English, a miracle play, is a kinde of interlude, compiled in Cornish out of some Scripture history, with that grossenes which accompanied the Romanes vetus Comedia. For representing it, they raise an earthen amphitheatre in some open field, having the Diameter of his enclosed playne some 40 or 50 foot. The Country people flock from all sides, many miles off to hear and see it; for they have therein devils and devices, to delight as well the eye as the eare; the players conne not their parts without booke, but are prompted by one called the Ordinary, who followeth at their back with the booke in his hand, and telleth them softly what they must pronounce aloud."

Writing a century and a half later than Carew, Dr. Borlase describes the amphitheatres in which these Cornish plays were given; more particularly one in the parish of St. Just near the Land's End. This round as it was popularly called, was "an exact circle of 126 feet in diameter; the perpendicular height of the bank, from the area within, now seven feet; but the height from the bottom of the ditch without, ten feet at present, formerly more. The seats consist of six steps, fourteen inches wide, and one foot high, with one on the top of all, when the rampart is about seven feet wide." Another round or amphitheatre was described by Dr. Borlase as a perfectly level area 130 feet across, and surrounded by an earthen mound eight feet high.

In such magnificent surroundings of open-air, picturesque country, sea, and sky, were these curious plays given to instruct and edify a multitude drawn at large from the country-side, which often must remain camped for two or three days in the neighbourhood to see the performances out.

IV.—From "The Cornish Drama," by Henry Jenner

(Celtic Review, April 1907)

"The trilogy known as the Ordinalia consists of:—(a) Origo Mundi, which begins with the Creation of the World, ... and ends with the building of Solomon's Temple; (b) Passio Domini, which represents the Temptation of Christ and the events from the Entry into Jerusalem to the Entombment; (c) Resurrectio Domini, which gives the story of the Harrowing of Hell, ... the Resurrection, and the events between the Resurrection and the Ascension with which it ends. Interpolated in the middle is the Legend of St. Veronica, and Tiberius, and the Death of Pilate. Running through all three is the old legend of the Origin of the Wood of the Cross." (Our two Mysteries are from "C").

V.—Contemporary Account of Sir David Lindsay's "Satire of the Three Estates"

(From a Letter Written by Sir Wm. Eure, 26th Jan. 1540)

"In the feast of Ephipane at Lightgowe, before the king, queene, and the whole counsaile, spirituall and temporall.—In the firste entres come in Solace (whose parte was but to make mery, sing ballets with his fellowes, and drink at the interluydes of the play), whoe showed firste to all the audience the play to be played. Next come in a king, who passed to his throne, having nae speche to thende of the play, and then to ratify and approve, as in Parliament, all things done by the rest of the players, which represented The Three Estates. With him came his cortiers, Placebo, Picthank, and Flatterye, and sic alike gard: one swering he was the lustiest, starkeste, best proportionit, and most valeyant man that ever was; and ane other swore he was the beste with long-bowe, crosse-bowe, and culverin, and so fourth. Thairafter there come a man armed in harness, with a swerde drawn in his hande, a Bushop, a Burgesman, and Experience, clede like a Doctor; who set them all down on the deis under the King. After them come a Poor Man, who did go up and down the scaffolde, making a hevie complainte that he was hereyet, throw the courtiers taking his fewe in one place, and his tackes in another; wherthrough he had sceyled his house, his wyfe and childrene beggyng thair brede, and so of many thousands in Scotland; saying thair was no remedy to be gotten, as he was neither acquainted with controller nor treasurer. And then he looked to the King, and said he was not king in Scotland, fore there was ane other king in Scotland that hanged Johne Armstrang, with his fellowes, Sym the Laird, and mony other mae; but he had lefte ane thing undone. Then he made a long narracione of the oppression of the poor, by the taking of the corse-presaunte beists, and of the herrying of poor men by the consistorye lawe, and of many other abusions of the Spiritualitie and Church. Then the Bushop raise and rebuked him. Then the Man of Armes alledged the contraire, and commanded the poor man to go on. The poor man proceeds with a long list of the bushop's evil practices, the vices of cloisters, etc. This proved by Experience, who, from a New Testament, shows the office of a bushop. The Man of Armes and the Burges approve of all that was said against the clergy, and alledge the expediency of a reform, with the consent of Parliament. The Bushop dissents. The Man of Armes and the Burges said they were two, and he but one, wherefore their voice should have most effect. Thereafter the King, in the play, ratified, approved, and confirmed all that was rehearsed."

THE END

Made in the USA
Las Vegas, NV
01 July 2022

50997754R00121